THE CHRISTIAN ENCOUNTERS

THE WORLD
OF POP MUSIC
AND JAZZ

WILLIAM ROBERT MILLER

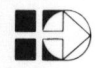

CONCORDIA
PUBLISHING
HOUSE
SAINT LOUIS

CONCORDIA PUBLISHING HOUSE, ST. LOUIS, MISSOURI
CONCORDIA PUBLISHING HOUSE LTD., LONDON, E. C. 1
COPYRIGHT 1965 BY CONCORDIA PUBLISHING HOUSE

LIBRARY OF CONGRESS CATALOG CARD NO. 65-16962

MANUFACTURED IN THE UNITED STATES OF AMERICA

CONTENTS

INTRODUCTION

Christians have seldom hesitated to form opinions about culture, and nowhere is this more true than in the field of popular music. There are those who frown on all secular music and those who indiscriminately applaud the latest fad, whatever it may happen to be, as "making a joyful noise unto the Lord." Rock-and-roll songs have been widely stigmatized as lascivious. In the 1920s, many guardians of white morality viewed both the Negro and his jazz music with ignorant suspicion; as late as 1938, Harry D. Gideonse, now president of Brooklyn College, insisted that "swing is musical Hitlerism."

Today popular music of all kinds is evidently here to stay. In an era of motion pictures, radio, and television the only way to avoid it is to retreat from the world. This we cannot do, for as Christians we are called to live and witness "in the world," even though not being conformed to it. Since this is the case, how shall we respond? Shall we yield to our casual impulses and let ourselves go — or manfully grit our teeth every time these sounds touch us?

These are only the very crudest questions posed by the Christian's encounter with popular music — and with that type of music which I have provisionally included in it: jazz. As we shall see, jazz is not merely one of several types of popular music. Part of our concern in this book will be to ask what makes it different and to discuss its special relationship to the Christian faith, to American and world culture.

Basic to all the questions that may be asked, however, is an underlying theological affirmation that cuts through any casual approach, whether of unthinking acceptance or rejection. Its first component is so obvious that we usually take it for granted and are tempted to forget its implications. This is the simple fact that the world in which we live is real, not an illusion, and the events that occur within it are purposeful. Coupled with this is the fact that the world does not just happen to be here; it is created by the same God who created man in His own image and who is the father of Jesus Christ. Throughout the Old Testament from Genesis on, it is made repeatedly clear that the whole realm of nature was created and intended for the good of all mankind, and that it is not static but structured as history and culture, the ways in which Biblical man responds to nature. Some religions are contented with a mythology dealing with imaginary or metaphorical events. But in the Bible, even angels are not depicted as part of a heavenly drama but as emissaries to men — not fictional characters but actual historic persons. Even when our faith ventures beyond fact, it is always rooted in it. The existence of Jesus is a fact without which the doctrine of the Incarnation would have no significance.

6

Indeed it is the continuity of our history as a church that obliges us to take the whole Bible seriously and keep re-examining its details in the light of archeological and linguistic research. It is a record of human events so empirically real that they point convincingly to the God who has a hand in them. Our leap of faith is not a mere stab in the dark, not a mere juggling of deified virtues, for the religious dimension is an extension of the secular. In a sense, God draws us out of the world, redeeming us from it, but this is by way of altering our perspective and our commitment, not our actual placement. We are not released from our relation to creation but rather assigned responsibility for it.

For creation implies freedom. Man is created not as a puppet but as a free being who can rebel against God and misuse the created world for his own selfish, distorted purposes. This rebellion against God and selfish misuse of His creation are what constitute sin in the proper meaning of the term, not the breaking of some set of mincing taboos. Sin represents the unhealthy side of created freedom. Through Christ the debilitating weight of sin is overcome, and man is redeemed for freedom in a positive way and reoriented to faithful obedience. By God's grace we respond in repentant faith and take part in the new being of Christ. In Christ, as the apostle Paul says, we become "a new creation." In Him the brokenness of sin is healed, and we are restored to our created wholeness. "Restored" may suggest a backward movement, but since history is real it is actually a forward step. Creation is not something old or aging, it is always new. If we refer back to Genesis, it is only to remind ourselves of what creation was like before the Fall and thus to recognize it when, in Jesus Christ, we see it redeemed.

Faith does not obliterate freedom; it does not remove the possibility of rebelliousness or of sin. Acceptance of

7

the lordship of Christ is not such an open-and-shut affair. It implies, rather, the use of freedom in God's service. As Luther put it, the Christian is free, subject to no one — and a servant, subject to everyone. His obedience is not that of a machine but of a free man who accepts responsibility. His fulfillment of that responsibility is not guaranteed; obedience is every day's option set over against the option of default and apostasy — we are in every moment free to serve God or to deny Him. The point is that in Christ we are no longer floundering and groping, for He shows us the way.

Our free response includes creative risk, and it is this which makes responsibility meaningful. We can see this most clearly in the transformation of personal relationships that undergirded the church in its earliest days, proceeding from Jesus' words: "Love one another as I have loved you." These words did not magically cause His followers to love one another. Moreover, anyone hearing these words could have replied: "I don't feel like it," or "No, I'll wait for others to love me first." Their response in obedience required faith; it meant going out on a limb, doing what they may have considered impossible. And without faith it would have been impossible, for only by the risk of faith could they have access to God's grace. There was something more than words or a "good idea" in Jesus' commandment; there was, above all, a new source of power and a norm for the exercise of their freedom. Jesus had shown them His love; they knew what He meant. But He also gave them the assurance that by God's grace and love in Him they, too, could love one another. Their risk in believing Him, in choosing obedience, was validated and transformed into the power to do His will. If Jesus had not been God the Son, that risk would have gone for nothing; it would have been sheer folly and those who undertook it the victims of a cruel joke. In fact, histori-

8

cally there were such people — for example, those who looked to Simon Magus for their salvation, risking their freedom in vain because God's grace and love were not in him. This simple fact speaks volumes of theology and underscores the radical truth of the church's claims about Jesus: by responding in faithful obedience His followers were given the power to do what He told them to do.

The church's record through the generations has been a spotty one; some Christians have wretchedly betrayed this commandment, while others have sacrificially shown their fidelity to it. But the norm remains valid as a touchstone of what the church really is — a fellowship of people bound to Christ in faith, expressing His creative, redemptive love. The responsibility which this implies, moreover, only begins within the church's fellowship; from there it reaches out into the world to embrace what is good and to cure what is broken. For the church is not a self-contained community of the perfected. It is a body of witnesses to the good news of Christ, but it remains a body of pardoned sinners, not superior beings. It is in the world that God's work is done.

"God's creation needs no completion," writes Karl Barth. "It was and is complete. But we can lose that completeness of creation, and we *have* lost it. It must be restored to us inalienably, by forgiveness and renewal." [1] Chief among the processes of renewal is what Barth calls "the work of culture" which embodies the promise of "fulfillment, unity, wholeness within [man's] sphere as creature, as man . . ." [2] "The work of culture takes its place among the earthly signs by which the church must make God's goodness, His friendship for men, visible to itself and to the world." [3]

Paul Tillich has given this observation a somewhat different emphasis:

In its prophetic role the church is the guardian who

9

reveals dynamic structures in society and undercuts their demonic power by revealing them, even within the church itself. In so doing, the church listens to prophetic voices outside itself, judging both culture and the church insofar as it is a part of the culture.[4]

To speak of prophetic voices within and outside the church in relation to culture is to speak of artistic creation, which is a reflection of what Barth means by the work of culture that contributes to the restoration of God's creation. Nikolai Berdyaev uses different terminology to indicate the "loss of completeness" which attenuates the free flow of full creation, interpreting this loss as the deadening effect of unfreedom:

> *Art is always a victory over the heaviness of "the world" — never adaptation to "the world." The act of art is directly opposed to every sort of added burden — in art there is liberation. The essential in artistic creativity is victory over the burden of necessity. . . . Every creative artistic act is a partial transformation of life.*[5]

Artistic creativity is not identical with God's creation, but it is an expression of it within the realm of culture, giving new life to whatever is stultifying and dross. Neither it nor culture itself has final value transcending history, but their value within history is real.

We do not approach these questions with a clean slate. Our approach to culture still tends to be clouded with a moralistic smugness inherited from the Victorian era, when "outward signs of an inward and spiritual grace" often became conventional signs of nothing more than worldly respectability. Lacking creative vitality itself, the church often adapted itself uncritically to the world in some ways while uttering officious denunciation in others. No proper Victorian lady or gentleman would consort with

10

publicans or ragtime pianists. Although such attitudes are waning today, there are still many church people suffering from a pride of "respectability" for which the Gospel provides no warrant, and who take it for granted that they are "better" than the unchurched beatnik. The fact is that Christ was crucified and resurrected for all mankind, including respectable church members and beatniks.

It is not the purpose of this book to suggest that standards be abolished or that we Christians blindly accept what we once blindly rejected. The world of culture is not the same as the world of nature, but even the latter is not all exquisite sunsets and noble stallions. As we distinguish between these and the disease germs that are also part of nature, we must also be prepared to sort out what is healthful and creative from what is dross or pernicious in the world of culture, specifically the world of pop music and jazz. All that we can say beforehand is that this world as such is part of the world we live in and with which we as Christians must be concerned. We must first accept it as such before we can explore it, understand it, and discover what is right and what is wrong within it.

This book is based on considerable study and research, some of it casually done over a period of years but much of it intensive and recent. I am indebted to all of the authors whose books and articles are mentioned in the footnotes and in the bibliography, as well as to many individuals such as the Rev. John G. Gensel, Edgar Summerlin, Alva I. Cox, Nat Hentoff, Laura Randall, Ed Douglas, and others with whom I had conversations or correspondence that added new material or insights and sometimes led to the correction of errors. Whatever flaws may remain are my own.

11

THE ROOTS OF JAZZ

Although jazz is a 20th-century product, its roots are as old as America itself, dating back to the arrival of the first African slaves in Virginia in 1619. For two centuries thereafter slave ships regularly brought to American ports thousands of captives, either directly from the West African coast or by way of the Caribbean. Even after the official ending of the slave trade in 1807, the importation of Africans continued illegally. As late as 1859 newly arrived Negroes were openly advertised for sale in Mississippi, and Stephen A. Douglas said that more were smuggled into the United States in that year than entered in any year when the slave trade was legal.

Until the eve of the Civil War, then, there was a steady stream of replenishment for African customs, folklore, and music that had earlier become transplanted and blended with Euro-American culture. In 1860 one out of every three persons living in the South was a Negro slave.

What was it like to be a slave? You worked hard all day in the hot sun, and if you were mistreated there was no way you could get justice; you were not a citizen. You could not travel unless your master shipped you somewhere. It was a crime for anyone to teach you to read and write. Even your wife and children were not your own. If you were a healthy male, you could be compelled to serve as a stud in the breeding of slave children just as a prize bull is hired out to sire calves. If you were an attractive woman, you might be used as an unwilling and unpaid prostitute by your white owner. You could be mercilessly beaten, your family scattered. The purpose of your existence was solely to benefit your master; accordingly, you were taught only as much English as he needed to tell you your tasks. Unlike the slaves of ancient Greece, you were treated as an animal or, at best, as a retarded child.

It was out of such a life that the Negro's music evolved. The fact is that he was neither subhuman nor childlike. He brought with him from Africa an already well-developed musical culture which anthropologists have only recently begun to understand. Field hollers, work chants, and spirituals were passed from one generation to the next with little change except the substitution of English for the various African dialects. According to Ernest Borneman, "Swing Low, Sweet Chariot," "River Jordan," and "One More River to Cross" were originally West African boat songs.

"The spirit," says a West African proverb, "will not descend without song." It is not surprising that vocal music took a preponderant place in the Negro's worship.

The church, moreover, was the slave's only authorized social meeting place. Amid the flux and uncertainty of individual and family life, it provided a measure of stability and continuity as well as an outlet for pent-up emotions. Although Christianity was first brought to him by white missionaries, its emphases became those that reflected his own lot — the Jesus who called out to those who labored and were heavy-laden, the Moses who led his people out of "Egypt land." Songs taken from white hymnals were subjected to African rhythms and harmonies, and new songs emerged directly from the hard life of these black Christians. Many of them have endured since Emancipation, and the tradition as a whole is preserved in unsophisticated Negro churches of the present day, with their shouts, spirituals, and gospel songs. The titles of some of these give some hint of their immediacy: "Jesus Is Real to Me," "Jesus on the Main Line," and "What Do You Think About Jesus? He's All Right!" The language is no special religious jargon, but that of everyday life.

Moreover, unlike the smooth concert arrangements familiar to white listeners, the spirituals as sung in the Negro church reflect a spontaneity and emotional aliveness that is largely traceable to West African tribal music, with its close relationship between language, rhythm, and timbre. Simple texts are given cumulative force not by melodic or harmonic development but by tone color, syncopated patterns of handclapping, riffs, "bluing" of notes, shifts of tempo, and other musical techniques that are far from "primitive" and in fact simply represent a culture with its own complexities that are very different from the European.

Emancipation and the Secular Blues

After Emancipation secular life began for the first time. A Negro could move from town to town, and although the church continued to play an important part in his life it was no longer the only place he could go for social life. It is generally believed that the blues as a separate art form arose in this period, probably growing out of the call-and-response pattern of much Negro church music, but undoubtedly influenced also by work songs. In form, the blues is a highly individual and improvised music, characterized by a stanza of three lines, the first two of which are identical. A man with a banjo or guitar would wander from place to place, singing at harvest picnics and clambakes or at roadside "jukes" — cheap, low-down saloons. He would sing the first verse, then repeat it as he thought up the last one. As in the church songs and perhaps even more, the blues' idiomatic strength is to be found in its expressiveness. The stress is not on individual style in a technical sense — not on the ability to embellish — but on the ability of the singer to communicate his feelings. The Negro blues singer *lives* what he is singing and may therefore deliberately choose harsh sounds when they are more expressive.

Parallel with the appearance of individual blues singers was the formation of country jug bands that played the blues on homemade instruments. In the towns and cities, Negro pianists in barrelhouses and gin mills imitated the syncopated guitar or banjo rhythms on their keyboards, producing not only the first piano blues but also ragtime and boogie-woogie, along with a variety of other forms: the stomp, the shuffle, the slow drag — all variants or aspects of the blues.

Another important development was the formation of concert and marching bands, frequently under the auspices of Negro fraternal lodges in such cities as New Orleans, Memphis, and St. Louis in the 1870s and after. With the increase of racial segregation toward the turn of the century, these organizations assumed increasing importance in Negro life.

Scott Joplin and Ragtime

Perhaps the career of Scott Joplin can provide a sketch of the era out of which jazz was to grow. Born in Texas in 1868, just three years after the end of the Civil War, he was the son of a railroad worker from North Carolina and a laundress from Kentucky who sang and played the banjo. As a child he showed musical aptitude. An old German music teacher gave him free lessons in piano technique, sight reading, and harmony.

In his early teens, after his mother died, Scott became in itinerant musician, roaming Texas, Louisiana, and the Mississippi Valley, playing in saloons, honky-tonks, tent shows — wherever work was to be found. Civil War songs, hollers, work songs, blues, jigs, and reels were all in the air. At 17 he landed in St. Louis in 1885, where he stayed for eight years, moving to Sedalia, Mo., in 1894 after forming a band and going to Chicago during the Columbian Exposition. In Sedalia he studied harmony and composition at George Smith College for Negroes, a Methodist institution, played second cornet in the Queen City Concert Band, and wrote his first music — a couple of Victorian ballads in waltztime. Joplin made a living by playing piano in saloons and bordellos in addition to his respectable concert band work and also formed a dance band (cornet, clarinet, baritone, tuba, and piano) to play at Negro social gatherings. During these years he began to write ragtime compositions, which achieved popularity both among the Negro community and in the saloons. In 1899 the first of these was published as "Original Rags." Though Joplin's first, it was preceded by two years by Tom Turpin's "Harlem Rag." In the decade that followed, many more appeared in print and were circulated widely wherever Negroes lived and eventually among whites.

Much the same happened elsewhere too. Often such

musicians as W. C. Handy found employment with minstrel bands, playing Sousa marches as they paraded to the public square and then cutting loose with a swingy version of current popular songs. Jack Laine turned from minstrel shows to form his Ragtime Band in 1900, abandoning the cakewalk, jig, and reel for the syncopated idiom. More than anywhere else, however, it was New Orleans that was to serve as the seedbed of jazz. For it was here, first of all, that musicians went beyond the limits of ragtime to add other elements derived from the blues tradition. Already at the turn of the century the marching bands of New Orleans Negro lodges were engaging in collective improvisation as they played such tunes as "When the Saints Go Marching In" at funerals.

The Birth of New Orleans Jazz

One of the earliest figures in jazz was Buddy Bolden. Born in 1878 in New Orleans, he was a member of a gospel-shouting church. Growing up in the era of brass bands and ragtime, he learned to play the cornet and organized the first out-and-out jazz band in 1900, specializing in playing the blues and in winning "carving contests" — feats of sustained improvisation in competition with another player.

Of the music generally, LeRoi Jones has observed: "The first instrumental voicings of New Orleans jazz seem to have come from the arrangements of the singing voices in the early Negro churches. . . . The Negro's religious music contained the same 'rags,' 'blue notes,' and 'stop times' as were emphasized later and to much greater extent in jazz." [1]

What happened in New Orleans with the advent of Buddy Bolden and others like him was the evolution of a style and a tradition distinct from, yet related to, the vocal blues, Negro church music, popular band music, and other influences. The musicians who took part in this evolution played in many places — on riverboats, in minstrel and marching bands — but from 1897 to 1917 their chief opportunities lay in the cabarets, gambling joints, and brothels of Storyville, the New Orleans tenderloin district. When it was closed in 1917, the musicians headed north in search of work, finding the way prepared by the earlier spread of ragtime, which by then had become a highly commercialized popular craze.

During the next five years or so Chicago took the place of New Orleans as the nation's jazz center. In 1917 a white group, the Original Dixieland Jazz Band, made the first recording of "Tiger Rag," to be followed in subsequent years by a number of other bands. One of these was the outstanding King Oliver's Creole Jazz Band, which arrived in Chicago in 1918 — the same year a young trumpeter, Louis Armstrong, joined Fate Marable's riverboat band. By 1920, the year of the first radio broadcast anywhere in the world, there were over 40 outstanding New Orleans jazzmen working in Chicago. In 1922 Armstrong joined King Oliver at the same time Fletcher Henderson was forming the first noteworthy jazz-influenced dance band in New York. Armstrong, one of the great virtuosos of jazz, exerted a powerful influence on the development of jazz style in its formative years, moving from Chicago in 1924 to join Fletcher Henderson and then forming his own Hot Five in 1925. Typical of the blues tradition, Armstrong treated his instrument as an extension of the voice to shout, wail, and sing in brass, challenging other soloists as well as the ensemble to respond in a manner analogous to the interplay of preacher and congregation in the Negro church. In fact certain types of playing were called "preaching the blues." His impact on the Henderson dance band and on a whole generation of jazzmen was considerable.

Beiderbecke and Ellington

But there were other, less frenetic currents at work. In contrast to Armstrong there was Bix Beiderbecke, a white trumpet player who, unable to master the blues idiom, developed a controlled, lyrical style of improvisation and helped to form the intense, driving "Chicago jazz" favored by white musicians of the period. Beiderbecke, who died in 1931 at the age of 28, has since become a legendary figure in the jazz of the 1920s.

Perhaps of equal importance with the Armstrong influence was Duke Ellington, who began his career as a ragtime pianist in Washington, D. C., in 1917. By 1923 he had formed a small band that played at the Kentucky Club in that city. Four years later, having absorbed a great deal from King Oliver and Louis Armstrong through key soloists, Ellington came to New York, where his orchestra was featured at the Cotton Club in Harlem. With the recording of "Black and Tan Fantasy" in that year (1927) Ellington established an enduring reputation as a serious composer within the jazz idiom. Based firmly on the blues and incorporating deliberate archaisms which instrumentally evoked the field holler, the "Fantasy" was an authentic tone poem of Negro life which featured a trumpet solo by Bubber Miley, echoing a church cantata, "Holy City," which his mother used to sing.

In the four decades that followed, Ellington wrote hundreds of tunes. Some were ephemeral swing ballads, but many, such as "The Mooche," "Mood Indigo," and "Take the A Train," attained the status of repertory pieces and were played by many jazz groups. The current catalog includes whole LPs of Ellington works played by various outstanding jazzmen,[2] and individual pieces are included on many others. Spanning a period of considerable change, Ellington has grown and absorbed the spirit of the times while preserving a continuity of style rooted in

19

the blues. In performance and in his compositions he has given scope to the unique styles of his instrumentalists, sometimes writing passages or entire works for outstanding soloists.

The Swing Era

The rise of the Ellington band signaled a new era — that of the big band with its emphasis on arrangements rather than improvisations, and often on danceability rather than freedom of expression. During the late 1920s, Paul Whiteman's orchestra created a type of dance music mildly tinctured with jazz elements and featuring occasional solos by Bix Beiderbecke and other white jazz musicians whom Whiteman discovered and hired. Another band, Ben Pollack's Park Central Orchestra, was closer to the jazz tradition; based in Chicago, it consisted of white musicians influenced by the New Orleans style. Out of these two bands came such men as Tommy and Jimmy Dorsey, Gene Krupa, and Benny Goodman. Goodman formed his own band in 1934, drawing many of these other white players into it. Equipped with a sheaf of Fletcher Henderson arrangements, Goodman soared to fame as "King of Swing." He found the right formula in a smoother blend of jazz and conventional dance band elements than Whiteman or Pollack had achieved. Most of his repertory consisted of syncopated versions of the popular ballads of the day, but he also cultivated jazz resources, copying from the Negro orchestras and even hiring such artists as Teddy Wilson, Charlie Christian, Buck Clayton, and Cootie Williams. Such Goodman players as Glenn Miller, Tommy Dorsey, Harry James, and Gene Krupa later formed their own swing bands, as did musicians influenced indirectly like Artie Shaw and Woody Herman.

Much of what they all played could scarcely be called jazz. By 1940 most jazz performers were smothered in

20

big-band commercial arrangements. Even the small swing ensemble such as Benny Goodman's trio, quintet, sextet, or septet, though offering the soloist more freedom and spontaneity, tended toward the slick superficiality of the pace-setting big band.

The Negro bands were not unaffected by the trend. Although groups like Fletcher Henderson's and Jimmie Lunceford's preserved traces of the blues idiom, it was most often carried on through creative soloists such as Coleman Hawkins, a saxophone player with Henderson since the early 1920s, who developed a style that challenged the trumpet as the paramount solo instrument of jazz.

It is generally agreed that swing itself contributed nothing to the evolution of jazz. The most memorable of Benny Goodman's performances were not the pop tunes, not the display pieces such as "Clarinade," but such numbers as "King Porter Stomp," a Storyville classic by Jelly Roll Morton, and "One O'Clock Jump" by Count Basie. Indeed, the emergence of Basie and his Kansas City band on the national scene soon after Goodman's debut as a bandleader was the first step toward the coming revolt against swing. For Basie's swing was very much ad-libbed, based on a large rhythm section, and much of his repertory consisted of refinements of the coarse rhythm-and-blues style from which popular rock and roll later originated. Basie, a native of New Jersey, had learned the Harlem "stride" style of piano playing from Fats Waller in New York and had gone to Kansas City in the late 1920s. His music was a blend of cosmopolitan sophistication and earthy blues.

Seeds of Revolt

Although Basie's comparative earthiness and blues-rooted warmth contrasted refreshingly with most other swing bands, this must not be mistaken for crudeness.

The first outstanding pioneer, sowing the seeds of revolt against swing, was Basie's tenor saxophonist Lester Young, who was unable to hold Coleman Hawkins' former position in Fletcher Henderson's band in 1934 because his tone was "too light." In many ways Young epitomized the best of both white and Negro jazz. A sensitive and intro-spective player who counted Bix Beiderbecke's delicate style among his formative influences, he also possessed a firm sense of the blues. His genius consisted chiefly in the freely developed improvisation of melody with intrinsic rhythmic interest, following the harmony of the tune on which he was improvising.

The revolt against swing came to fruition in the early 1940s in Harlem jam sessions where young big-band side-men gathered to play experimentally in small groups. Tired of the restrictions imposed on them by the big-band arrangements, which limited solo opportunities to established star performers like Coleman Hawkins and trumpeter Roy Eldridge, they sought to explore to the fullest the resources of their respective instruments and recapture the spontaneity of the early blues. Following Lester Young, they evolved new concepts of time and of the relationship between rhythm and melody. A decisive development, fathered by Kenny Clarke and carried for-ward by Max Roach, was the abandonment of the bass pedal in drumming and the shift from a staccato beat to a legato sound produced with the top cymbal, freeing the drummer to improvise accents against the basic beat, which was softened and given to the string bass. The dominant innovators were saxophonist Charlie Parker, a native of Kansas City, and Dizzy Gillespie, a brilliant young trumpeter from South Carolina. Even more than the earliest New Orleans jazz, the bebop style, which emerged about 1944, was a soloist's music in which unison playing was all but eliminated. Pop ballads were turned upside down and inside out in improvised paraphrases and harmonic refurbishings, and many original tunes suited to the bop idiom were created, often arising out of an inspired improvising session. The blues influence is clear both in the feeling and in the form of performance and composition alike. Such works as "Billie's Bounce" (Parker), "A Night in Tunisia" (Gillespie), and "Round About Midnight" (Thelonious Monk) have become jazz classics. Arrangements were not wholly abandoned — to do so would have imposed a formidable challenge — but they were liberated from their former rigidity. Increasingly, use was made of "head" arrangements — memorizations of orally assigned parts. Even when expressed in written charts, they were more like sketches than full orchestrations, and each player was counted on to exercise his freedom to create and express himself.

The impact of the bop revolt can hardly be overstressed. From the start it signified the renewal of jazz by blues-rooted Negro musicians who rescued it from the white commercialism implicit in swing. But it also heralded a new interracialism predicated on the acceptance of the Negro idiom as normative rather than a stockpile from which to replenish "white" musical ideas.

As a distinct style, bop flourished from about 1945 to 1955; the "bop era" came to a close with the death of Charlie Parker. But its influences were felt throughout the jazz world. After 1945 swing musicians either absorbed the bop style, as did Woody Herman, or they went commercial — or ceased to play. A number of white musicians rejected both swing and bop to revive the early New Orleans style, often insisting that their nostalgic cult of "Dixieland," actually born in the 1940s, was the only "pure" jazz — a notion paralleling that of modern Bach or Mozart fanciers who repudiate contemporary classical music.

Progressive and Cool Jazz

The most significant departure from bop was the advent of the "cool" style in 1948. Even before bop had fully taken shape, West Coast white musicians had begun their own attempts to break out of the limits of swing. As early as 1944, Stan Kenton in Los Angeles had begun to move away from the Jimmie Lunceford style he formerly had copied, and by 1946 he was trying to infuse his big band with a new "progressive jazz" idiom influenced by the classical concert hall and featuring such compositions as "Artistry in Rhythm," which departed radically from the 32-bar ballad form that dominated swing. In almost every way, progressive jazz was the diametrical opposite of bop; it stressed the big band, detailed formal composition, and a conscious affinity with concert music. Briefly Kenton had an imitator in Boyd Raeburn, whose specialties included "Boyd Meets Stravinsky," but Raeburn eventually returned to commercial swing. Despite the difference in orientation, however, Kenton's musicians readily responded to many of the bop influences. Other white musicians, such as Claude Thornhill and Lennie Tristano, were also trying in less spectacular ways to achieve a new jazz sound.

In 1948 the 21-year-old Miles Davis, trumpeter of the Charlie Parker Quintet, brought some of these strands together in an ensemble made up in large part of musicians from the Kenton and Thornhill bands, most of them in their early 20s. The cool style which this interracial group introduced appropriated the new freedom of bop to a restrained, detached style of expression somewhat in the manner of Beiderbecke and Lester Young; it went in for muted sonorities in contrast with the jagged frenzies of bop. Many of the musicians in Davis' short-lived group were later to make a significant contribution to jazz in the 1950s — Gerry Mulligan, Kai Winding, Lee Konitz,

Gunther Schuller, Max Roach, and John Lewis. Besides Davis himself, who dominated the music of the decade with his lean, controlled trumpet tone, John Lewis became especially noted as a composer and leader of the Modern Jazz Quartet, achieving a unique fusion of spontaneous improvisation and such formal devices as the classical fugue, and developing a repertory that included works by such diverse composers as Dizzy Gillespie and Heitor Villa Lobos as well as originals ranging from the swinging "Bluesology" to the delicate "Vendôme."

The MJQ began recording in 1950, soon after the first Miles Davis "Birth of the Cool" recordings, but it did not become a regular performing ensemble until 1954. Others capitalized on the new idiom before then — first, the quintet of English-born pianist George Shearing, who impressed jazz critics in 1949 but soon afterward deteriorated into a producer of commercial "satin sounds." Second came Dave Brubeck. Classically trained like John Lewis, Brubeck never approached the kind of synthesis which Lewis achieved, but his use of classical forms and allusions to adorn a bouncy, riff-based jazz style brought him great popularity among college audiences, first on the West Coast and later throughout the country. After his quartet's debut on the national scene in 1954, however, Brubeck rapidly deteriorated; within a few years he was coasting along on clichéd arrangements tailored to the commercial market and only partly redeemed by the sensitive solos of the quartet's featured altoist, Paul Desmond. It remained for less popular men like Gerry Mulligan to carry on the creative impulse of the cool school among serious white jazz musicians. In 1952 Mulligan took the revolutionary step of forming a quartet without piano, relying on bass and drums alone to undergird trumpet and his own baritone saxophone. Another cool pioneer was Stan Getz, a sax player with Woody Herman's band, who developed a style based on Lester Young's.

Return to the Roots

Reacting against the cool were a cluster of styles that could be called "neo-bop." Beginning about 1954, Negro jazzmen such as Art Blakey and Horace Silver inaugurated a vigorous affirmation of the historic roots of jazz, going back to the primitive country blues and to the gospel songs and shouts of the grassroots Negro church, stripping away all Europeanisms in a quest for the unalloyed emotional expressiveness of the basic blues, which they then harnessed to the music techniques of bop. Some of the resulting styles were "soul jazz," "hard bop," and "funky jazz," each stressing individual elements — religious fervor with sounds of preaching and shouting evoked instrumentally, the application of strong rhythmic accents to standard bop material, or the frank sexuality of the secular man-woman blues.

During the 1960s jazz has continued to undergo a rich evolution. None of its rival tendencies has won out, nor have they become cultish. There has been a striking degree of interaction between them as well as growth from within. Miles Davis, while perfecting his individual style, has become less determinedly cool, applying his sensitive lyricism with equal effectiveness to hard bop, to sentimental ballads, to Spanish flamenco music, and to his own cool jazz compositions. John Coltrane, one of the outstanding tenor sax players of today, was a member of Davis' quintet in the late 1950's. Another, Sonny Rollins, was identified with neo-bop; in 1959 he withdrew from public appearances for two years to rethink his style. Both have been influenced by the avant-garde Ornette Coleman, a younger man who endured poverty and ridicule in pursuit of his own artistic vision of absolute freedom in improvisation.

Charles Mingus, one of the most creative of today's jazzmen, moves with equal ease among classical influences, bop, and the work of Ellington. His own compositions are fresh and far-ranging, but his greatest strength undoubtedly is in his mastery of the blues and gospel idiom. He is also an extraordinary bassist and a highly gifted improviser.

Among the significant white jazzmen of today are clarinetist Jimmy Giuffre, pianist Bill Evans, and composer Edgar Summerlin, each of whom, as well as the Negro pianist Cecil Taylor and composer-pianist George Russell, has engaged in provocative attempts to extend the frontiers of jazz without abandoning its essence. Giuffre has introduced atonality into jazz in a striking way. Evans has brought a precise pianistic technique to bear on unrehearsed improvisations that call for great resourcefulness among the members of his trio; although spontaneous, the result combines authentic feeling with a wide range of carefully chosen pianistic devices that can withstand critical scrutiny. Summerlin has explored the principle of indeterminacy in jazz as Stockhausen and Boulez have done in classical music. Russell, who was closely associated with the bop movement in 1946, subsequently moved ahead as both theorist and composer, developing a pantonal "Lydian concept of tonal organization," which serves as a basis for some of today's most vital jazz. Among both the newest and youngest of white jazzmen are flutist Jeremy Steig and pianist Denny Zeitlin, both of whom in their early 20s show a marked individuality as well as some indebtedness to diverse influences such as Rollins, Monk, and Evans. Zeitlin, who first appeared on a recording while a medical student at Johns Hopkins, has not only impressed critics with his creative drive and discipline at the keyboard but has also shown promise as a composer in an idiom related to Russell's. Steig, making his recorded debut in 1964 not long before the tragic death of Eric Dolphy, one of the decade's most creative Negro saxophonists, has already displayed a kinship with

27

the latter's highly expressive use of the flute, an instrument which has only recently begun to find its place in jazz. Again, as in so many other instances, these white players have drawn discernible strengths from the Negro tradition and fused them with other elements from outside it. Nowadays, however, it is less a matter of copying or "raiding" and more a tutelage of integrity. Despite severe problems of gaining a hearing, younger musicians manage to exert their influence. The most forceful "new voices" include such men as Archie Shepp, John Tchicai, and Andrew Hill, all Negroes.

Jazz in the 1960s has transcended its origins and withstood the assaults of commercialism, reaffirming its roots as a music of Negro origin while reaching out to embrace the world. In the great diversity it was possible for such a man as Thelonious Monk, a participant in the earliest bop jam sessions, to exert a legendary but marginal influence for over two decades, while quietly adhering to his own unique style, and then suddenly to be discovered and catapulted to national prominence in 1963; and for another great artist, Bud Powell, equally a legend, to languish in a Paris hospital with tuberculosis and be forgotten until his reemergence in 1965 — significantly with a recording titled *A Portrait of Thelonious*.

The International Scene

Among the events of the 1950s and 1960s were Dizzy Gillespie's adventure in Afro-Cuban jazz and the more recent explorations of contemporary African music, which introduced such dances as the limbo and highlife to America and led the Liberian Government to commission Randy Weston to compose jazz works on African themes. At the same time Americans like Stan Getz and Charlie Byrd introduced the bossa nova, a new idiom arising from the transplanting of jazz to the Brazilian musical scene.

For many years jazz has been growing in Europe and

the Far East. A day's browsing in a New York record shop might turn up such groups as the Australian Jazz Quintet, Jorgen Ryg (Denmark), Bert Dahlander (Sweden), Johnny Dankworth (England), Toshiko Akiyoshi (Japan), the Basso-Valdambrini Octet (Italy), and Rolf Huhn, a clarinetist who fled East Germany in 1952 to form a jazz quartet in West Berlin. In 1964 the first recording of a Czech jazz group led by Karel Krautgartner was issued in the United States, joining the 1960 Polish ensemble of Jerzy Herman and the Skowronski Seven.

In the Soviet Union jazz has been officially stigmatized for decades as "bourgeois degeneracy." Despite hints of treason, however, Soviet jazzmen succeeded in the summer of 1962 in launching a School of Jazz in Leningrad, where trumpeter Konstantin Nosov and alto saxophonist Gennady Golstein sought ways of moving out from the styles of Charlie Parker and Miles Davis to a distinctively Russian jazz based on the *chastushki* folk style instead of the blues. During the same year an international jazz festival was held in Warsaw. Listening to Soviet guitarist Nikolai Gromin there, an American said his playing sounded "like a country blues player who studied with Prokofiev."

The continuing vitality and growing international appeal of jazz is no accident. It is a music of creative expression, a voice of freedom. It will make itself heard wherever there are men to create it, wherever freedom is cherished.[3]

THE RISE OF POP MUSIC

Popular music is essentially a city phenomenon. As far back as the Middle Ages and well into the 19th century, urban musicians drew upon the traditional styles and patterns of rural folk songs and dances, adapting the originals for city use and composing new ones in the transplanted idiom. Sometimes, as in the Allemande, Ländler, and Deutsche Tänze, they were raised to the level of high art by such composers as Bach, Mozart, and Schubert. With the coming of the Industrial Revolution and the introduction of inexpensive printing methods, however, it became possible for enterprising tunesmiths to produce music not as an art but as a trade, selling their wares for a few pennies a copy to the general public. Thus London's Grub Street in the 1750s planted the first seeds of a music that was not only appealing to uncultivated ears but commercial — for the penny ballads proved their worth not by gradual acceptance but by sales as quick and as wide as 18th-century advertising methods could make them.

In America, the first settlers brought with them the ballads, jigs, reels, and flings of the British Isles, and in some rural areas they have changed little since the era of Shakespeare and Purcell. In the cities of colonial America, the English ballad became the archetype for commercial songs written for sale to the local populace.

Unique to American life, however, as we have already noted, was the Negro slave with his own distinctive folkways and forms of musical expression. The evolution of an Afro-American music, resulting in the blues and jazz, had a strong impact on the mainstream of Euro-American popular culture.

From Ballad Opera to Blackface

As early as 1769 Negroes had been caricatured on the stage by white performers who blackened their faces and imitated what they considered the comical and primitive antics of Afro-American song and dance. But the staple of musical entertainment continued to be the popular English ballad opera, typified by John Gay's *The Beggar's Opera*. It was not until 1828 in Baltimore that a popular entertainer, Thomas Rice, introduced the first major blackface act, "Jump Jim Crow." A dozen years later, such acts had multiplied and came to be grafted onto the ballad opera form, heralding the first distinctively American musical stage. In 1843 a four-man troupe calling themselves the Virginia Minstrels made their debut at New York's Chatham Square Theater. Among them was Dan Emmett, a circus drummer from Ohio who had been influenced by Thomas Rice. Some of the songs he wrote for the increasingly popular minstrel shows have become part of the repertory of today's folk singers — "The Blue-Tail

Fly," "Jim Crack Corn," "Old Dan Tucker," and "Dixie." Another Negro-inspired song of disputed authorship was "Zip Coon," better known today as "Turkey in the Straw." These and many other songs, such as "Buffalo Gals" and "Polly Wolly Doodle," were lighthearted, boisterous, and nonsensical. The melodies almost invariably were adaptations of English or Irish dance tunes. The words were at first lifted intact from actual Negro songs, some of which employed techniques not unlike those in Aesop's fables to express hidden meanings in a seemingly nonsensical way. To the white adapters, however, who could not penetrate the meaning, this nonsense quality seemed merely proof of the Negro's inferior status as a stupid buffoon. When the white minstrels wrote their own lyrics for "Negro" songs in imitation of this nonsense, it was *really* nonsense. But it was also a lot of fun for the listeners — for the same reasons that children delight in Mother Goose rhymes or the verses of Edward Lear.

At the same time, the minstrel shows provided a form of cultural expression through which to discharge feelings of guilt and anxiety about the institution of slavery and, after the Civil War, about the still unresolved racial cleavage which slavery had imposed. The blackface show was popular partly because it depicted the Negro "in his place" as the white man saw it and because exhibiting a facsimile of those in bondage as "contented darkies" made it possible for the whites to evade a moral issue that has only begun to be faced in the 1960s. The actual Negro otherwise had virtually nothing to do with the first minstrel shows. Performers, song writers, and accompanists all were white, as were the audiences. They used a Negro musical instrument, the banjo, and burnt-cork makeup to create a fantasy and frequently an outright lie based more on wishful thinking than on fact.

The minstrel songs were presented on stage along with

gags, dances, burlesque skits, and choral numbers. From these burlesque, vaudeville, the musical variety show, the review and extravaganza were eventually to grow, culminating in the Broadway musical of today. But meanwhile the minstrel show and its sentimental stereotypes continued to dominate American popular music.

Master of Minstrelsy

Stephen Foster, America's first great song writer, was profoundly influenced both by the blackface stage and by childhood visits to a Negro church. Born near Pittsburgh in 1826, as a youth Foster liked to imitate the minstrels' performance of "Zip Coon" and "Jump Jim Crow." Although his first published song was a sentimental ballad in the English style, "Open Thy Lattice, Love," he soon began writing in the idiom of blackface — "Oh! Susannah," "Lou'siana Belle," and "Camptown Races," which were featured by such groups as the Ed Christy Minstrels and quickly gained nationwide popularity. Many of these melodies, according to anthropologist Ernest Borneman, were lifted almost unchanged from Negro riverboat chanteys — "Camptown Races" was originally "Sing and Heave"; some are even traceable to West Africa.[1]

At first Foster was reluctant to have his name associated with such pieces because he wanted to make his mark as a composer of "refined" ballads. So diffident was he about this, in fact, that his first masterpiece, "Swanee River," was published in 1851 under Ed Christy's name. With its tremendous success, however, Foster resigned himself to the inevitable and went on to write such favorites as "My Old Kentucky Home" and "Massa's in the Cold, Cold Ground," exploiting the resources of the ballad style in the service of the minstrel show. Combining a natural melodic gift with a sentimental strain of melancholy, these songs had an immense appeal as a com-

33

plement to the humorous nonsense songs. The fantasy scenes which they described were sheer concoctions. Foster did not have a Kentucky home, nor did he ever see the Suwanee River — he chose, and in the latter case changed, these names for the euphonious sound. The element of nostalgic yearning and romantic daydreaming was the fruit of an unhappy marriage which ultimately incapacitated him as a song writer and led him, through alcoholism, to a life of sordid poverty on the Bowery in New York, where he died in 1864 at the age of 38. It was out of his frustrations that he wrote such songs as "Jeanie with the Light Brown Hair" (to his wife, who disliked music and wanted him to give up songwriting) and "Beautiful Dreamer." His last successful Negro-oriented song, "Old Black Joe," was about a slave owned by his wife. Most of his last compositions were "white" ballads and nearly all of them were flops.

Foster was outstanding in his melodic gift and there was deep sincerity of emotion in what he wrote, even though he falsified and fabricated the terms in which it was expressed. He did not begin by writing for a market, but he found that success lay along the path of the black-face shows and capitalized on this fact.

Songs Written to Order

In Foster's time the publication of songs and their subsequent popularization was very much a matter of chance. Until the 1890s, song publishers were scattered among half a dozen cities from coast to coast, and song writers had great difficulty reaching the public unless they had contacts with the stage or were themselves minstrel show or vaudeville performers. It was in fact one of the latter who did much to change this situation. As a boy, Charles K. Harris earned his living in Milwaukee vaudeville theaters, playing the banjo and singing minstrel songs.

34

He also wrote a number of songs geared to specific performers and their styles or to a specific scene in a show. Some of these were used, but he did not make any money this way.

Harris decided next to open an office and publish his own songs. He posted a sign, "Songs Written to Order," and set about the business of devising compositions that would have strong market qualities. Often these were based on incidents in daily life either witnessed by himself or taken from newspaper clippings and then lavishly embellished into a highly improbable story cast in ballad form, involving sentimentalized lovers' quarrels, heart-rending situations of mistaken identity, a lost child or other "human interest" tales calculated to tug at the listener's emotions. In a few years, Harris scored his first great success when his story ballad, "After the Ball," was introduced on a vaudeville stage in 1892. The sheet music, published by Harris, sold five million copies.

By this time, music publishers had already begun to move their offices to New York in the vicinity of Union Square, which had become a bustling entertainment center, the site of Tony Pastor's Music Hall, Lüchow's restaurant, the Academy of Music, and various dance halls, burlesque houses, and saloons. Seeing the opportunity for exploitation, Harris moved to this locale. By the mid-1890s, others with the same idea were also flourishing. To the story ballad was added every conceivable type of song and the formula by which to concoct it. These formulas, according to David Ewen, were "so efficacious that most often these songs were created by composers who did not know how to write a note of music." [2]

Few opportunities were missed. When President Grover Cleveland's marriage to Frances Folsom was in the offing, one firm was ready with "President Cleveland's Wedding March," and the public obliged by responding with a nationwide demand for the sheet music. This is one of the clearest early examples of the popular song as a commodity produced in anticipation of a demand. With the waning of the minstrel show as a staple of entertainment, the market for blackface music was given a new lease through the introduction of the "coon song." Unlike the ministrel song, the new genre used syncopated rhythms borrowed from the blues. In a few years its popularity led to the introduction of something closer to jazz. With such titles as "All Coons Look Alike to Me," the coon songs were highly offensive to Negroes. Whether their initial appeal was primarily in the racial lampoon or in the catchy rhythm, the coon songs soon gave way to the ragtime tunes of Negro composers Scott Joplin and Tom Turpin. In the years to follow, their style was copied by the commercial music mills and blended into the conventional ballad idiom to create yet another market.

In addition to these, there were songs written for the immigrant market, such as "Down Went McGinty" and "My Wild Irish Rose," novelty songs such as Harris' "Hello Central, Give Me Heaven," capitalizing on the beginnings of widespread use of the telephone, humorous jingles, and whatever else could be sold.

Carrying Harris' philosophy to its logical conclusion, the Union Square publishers did not leave their markets to chance. Not only did they advertise in theatrical journals; they sent "song pluggers" to local sheet music stores to play their tunes on the piano. At night they made the rounds of the saloons and theaters, singing and playing and buttonholing vaudeville performers and band leaders. They went through the streets in trucks with megaphones, and for two decades it was a common practice in movie houses for song pluggers to put on a community sing with slides that illustrated the lyrics that were printed on them.

Tin Pan Alley

At the turn of the century, as the theatrical district moved uptown, the center of the popular music industry shifted from Union Square to West 28th Street, a street better known to the music world as Tin Pan Alley, so named by a newspaper reporter for the tinny sound of a piano he heard in the office of a music publisher. The change of locale brought few changes in the kind of music being produced; the big names in popular music — George M. Cohan, Victor Herbert, Sigmund Romberg, and others — were primarily associated with the Broadway stage rather than with the publishers, though of course their music brought millions of dollars to Tin Pan Alley. In partial contrast to the catch-as-catch-can concept of "songs written to order," the leading Broadway composers were adept in the "light classical" European tradition of Offenbach, Suppé, Märschner, and Johann Strauss and possessed the musical skills necessary to carry it on in America. In addition to his many operettas, Victor Herbert, for example, was capable of writing a cello concerto. None of his work was original or profound, but it was full of melodic ideas and had a freshness and romantic charm that was sorely lacking in much of the Tin Pan Alley output. Not surprisingly, Herbert himself was not an American product. Born in Dublin, he received his musical training in Germany at the Stuttgart Conservatory. Half a dozen of the other top "American" operetta composers were born in Germany. Rudolf Friml came from Prague, Sigmund Romberg from Austria-Hungary. The characteristic plots and settings of their music were fabulous and far removed from the American scene, using such locales as Arabia, Vienna, or some mythical European land where schmaltz was king. Unlike earlier American theatrical productions such as *The Black Crook*, many of the works of Herbert, Friml, and Romberg attained the status of classics; such operettas as *The Student Prince* and *Rose Marie* have long outlived the period in which they were written, and if Herbert's stage works have not survived, many of the songs he wrote for them are still favorites.

These composers represent an intrusion rather than a development in American popular music. Yet in addition to the legacy of their songs, they are important for the jolt they gave to the complacent hucksters of formula-made music, if only by revealing a more sophisticated kind of formula and tapping an unsuspected market for music of light classical pretensions. In so doing, they challenged Tin Pan Alley to come forth with what is probably the greatest outpouring of creativity in the history of pop music.

Ragtime had already made its appearance, but not without opposition from some quarters. In 1899 *The Musical Courier* termed it "vulgar, filthy, and suggestive," and a 1901 resolution of the American Federation of Musicians pledged its members to make every effort to suppress this "trash," which conjured up visions of loose-living Negroes abandoning themselves to sensual pleasures unthinkable to the Victorian mind, which treasured the docility of "Old Black Joe" and the sexless reveries of "Thine Alone" and "One Kiss." Not that ragtime was intrinsically bawdy — its rhythms could be found in the Negro church, praising the Lord with unashamed religious fervor. But ragtime tunes as such did in fact come to Tin Pan Alley from honky-tonk saloons and from the Negro whorehouses of New Orleans and St. Louis, and the lyrics were earthy enough to scandalize the prim custodians of Victorian morality.

White Ragtime

It was a Jewish immigrant from Russia named Israel Baline who made the major breakthrough. Beginning as a teen-age saloon singer, Baline worked his way up to become a song plugger and then a lyricist on the staff of a Tin Pan Alley firm, writing ditties for vaudeville acts. In 1910, having changed his name to Irving Berlin, he wrote a song called "Alexander's Ragtime Band," which managed to capture the swingy syncopation of the Negro idiom without the "roughness" of the honky-tonk atmosphere. Within months the song sold a million copies, and virtually every songwriter in the business scrambled to cash in on the new market it had opened up. It temporarily eclipsed every other type of popular music and had a radical effect on American habits of social dancing. The easy rhythms superseded the more taxing waltz and polka and were responsible for the opening of the first night clubs in 1911. "Everybody's Doin' It," said the title of another of Berlin's many ragtime tunes. And everybody was.

About this time, a twelve-year-old Brooklyn boy named George Gershwin began learning the piano classics of Chopin, Debussy, and Ravel. The boy responded enthusiastically to the ragtime craze and later got a job as staff pianist with a Tin Pan Alley publisher. Jerome Kern was another young American who underwent a similar apprenticeship. Together they and others like them revolutionized not only the shape of the popular song but also the American musical theater. A comparison of Kern's *Show Boat* of 1927 with the minstrel shows of Foster's time would show both continuity and growth. Its hit song, "Old Man River," like some of Foster's ballads, has been mistaken for a traditional Negro song.

The ragtime influence was barely noticeable in many of the sentimental tunes that emerged from Tin Pan Alley during its heyday in the 1910s and 1920s, but the simplicity and directness of the ragtime style doubtless contributed something that carried over into the ballad. Berlin had barely begun to enjoy fame as the "king of ragtime" when his bride of a few months died of typhoid. Out of his grief Berlin wrote "When I Lost You," the first of many ballads that are still prized for their tenderness and un-feigned emotional expression. His second marriage in 1926 was preceded by ballads of courtship such as "Always" and followed by more love songs like "How Deep Is the Ocean."

The "Jazz Age" in Popular Music

Having absorbed ragtime into its musical mainstream, America was ready, at the end of World War I, for further adventures. The so-called "Jazz Age," which was more than simply a musical phenomenon, was the product of many complex factors — the disillusionment of many young Americans after the carnage of the war and their quest for new styles of life, the advent of the phonograph and the radio, the new cultural climate arising from en-counter between Europe and America, Europe's discovery of African art (the logical next step after Gauguin's Poly-nesia). Certainly a key factor, too, was the rapid migra-tion of Negro jazz up the Mississippi from New Orleans to Chicago. Ragtime had scarcely been appropriated by Tin Pan Alley when it died out as a jazz style — or more accurately grew into new and different styles. As jazz moved out from New Orleans, it gathered small numbers of white musicians, such as Bix Beiderbecke, who set up jazz bands and developed their own styles based on what they heard the Negroes play. Often the white jazzmen played the same tunes, but they lacked the blues feeling and substituted spectacular technique for the Negroes' immediacy of expression.

At a still farther remove from real jazz was the ragtime-oriented musician Paul Whiteman, who was attracted by jazz but unable to muster the degree of spontaneity neces-sary for the improvisations that gave this music much of its power and vitality. Thus, while both Negro and white jazz musicians continued to develop a distinct idiom during the following decades, there was a parallel development in the pop music of Tin Pan Alley and Broadway. Band leaders like Whiteman visited clubs where jazz was played and went back to their own bandstands with orchestrations and arrangements that reproduced in greatly modified form something of the sweet-and-hot flavor of jazz. These syncopated borrowings were far from the player-created blues, but their written-down limitations were alleviated often by the inclusion of jazz soloists like Beiderbecke in Whiteman's orchestra. Whiteman's influence may be credited with much of the fluidity of the musical scene of the 1920s that increasingly blurred the boundaries between pop music and jazz. By the early 1930s there had emerged a new style of music called swing, built on the overlap between blues-derived improvisations and the post-ragtime pop ballad.

Swing Bands and Pop Ballads

The ballad itself partook of the jazz influence in its freshness and casualness of expression. If the more clearly jazz side of swing was represented by the soloist-bandleader such as Benny Goodman, the Dorsey brothers, Harry James, Artie Shaw, and Woody Herman, the clearly pop side of it can best be seen in the songs that emerged from the Broadway stage of the 1920s and 1930s as well as from the early Hollywood musical films. Gershwin's "Fascinating Rhythm" and "The Man I Love," both written in 1924, have endured for 40 years, showing respectively the catchy fast rhythms and the "blue mood" typical of the swing ballad. In the decade that followed, Gershwin wrote such melodies as "Someone to Watch over Me," "'S Wonderful," "Embraceable You," "I Got Rhythm," "Strike Up the Band," and "Summertime," to mention only some of those most frequently heard today.

Another major figure of the Jazz Age was Cole Porter, whose songs are unsurpassed for their saucy urbanity —

41

"Night and Day," "I Get a Kick Out of You" and "What Is This Thing Called Love," among others. Space does not allow more than brief mention of the many swing composers who, chiefly in the 1930s, made permanent contributions to pop music: Jerome Kern ("Yesterdays"), Vernon Duke ("April in Paris"), Richard Rodgers ("My Funny Valentine"), Vincent Youmans ("Tea for Two"), Jimmy McHugh ("I Can't Give You Anything but Love"), Harold Arlen ("That Old Black Magic"), Kurt Weill ("September Song"), and others. One of Hoagy Carmichael's songs, "Star Dust," was originally written as a fast-tempo piano rag and did not catch on until it was slowed down and sweetened with a sentimental orchestral arrangement, with words to match. During the same period more than a few songs also came from the world of jazz to become fixtures in the pop repertory — Fats Waller's "Honeysuckle Rose," Duke Ellington's "Solitude," and W. C. Handy's "Memphis Blues" among them. Typical of the interplay of the worlds of jazz and pop music during the heyday of swing was the use by jazz singer Billie Holiday of such Tin Pan Alley songs as Arthur Freed's "I Cried for You" and Ralph Rainger's "I Wished on the Moon." These and other ballads like them did not become standards but were long remembered as vehicles for the artists who sang or played them.

The Technological Revolution

In 1920 there was only one radio station in the United States — KDKA, Pittsburgh — and only a few thousand crystal sets. By 1928, seven million radios had been sold and nearly a thousand transmitters were operating, with approximately two-thirds or more of their total air time devoted to "harmony and rhythm" as purveyed by such groups as the Happiness Boys, the Ipana Troubadours, the A & P Gypsies, and Rudy Vallee. This fact, combined with the advent of the first motion pictures to use recorded

42

sound, the pinch of the Depression, and the proliferation of inexpensive recordings, rapidly and radically changed the music industry at the same time that swing was coming into vogue. In part the changes may account for the sharp drop in the output of enduring hits after 1940. It is a fact of the current musical scene that very few of the songs heard today date back five or ten years. Either they are new songs, fresh from the factory, or they may date as far back as a quarter of a century or more.

The technological revolution begun by radio and capped with the long-playing record and television placed the performer in the national spotlight. In 1910 people had little choice between playing "Alexander's Ragtime Band" themselves or hearing it performed by whatever musicians happened to be in town. By 1935 they could choose to hear Bing Crosby sing this tune or another one simply by turning on the phonograph, even if they lived in the middle of the Everglades. And if they were in any doubt about which of the available recordings to buy, they had only to turn on the radio to hear a wide variety of selections. Before long the publication of sheet music ceased to be of importance to the music publishers, who came to depend for their increasingly lucrative existence on royalties from the sale of records and of broadcasting and film rights.

Hollywood's rise meant Tin Pan Alley's fall. The three major music publishers were bought out by Warner Brothers for ten million dollars, and others were absorbed by rival filmmakers, leaving Mills Music and a few other smaller publishing houses in today's successor to Tin Pan Alley, the Brill Building in New York City.

Disk Jockeys and Juke Boxes

Before radio, it took time, even with the most vigorous promotional efforts, for a new pop tune to exhaust its sales potential. The life of a hit was well over a year. By the

43

1950s there were some 22 million phonographs in America's homes to be supplied with an endless succession of hits, each with a life span of no more than a few weeks. The role of the radio disk jockey had by this time shifted from that of a librarian to an ardent huckster of perishable, fast-moving goods. As early as 1935 the weekly radio show, "Hit Parade," told listeners the songs they should know if they wanted to be among the majority of their peers. The initial popularity of a record thus became a means to its further popularization. A song that stood no chance of becoming a hit was not worth bothering with, and only those that became hits had a chance of becoming smash hits.

The debasement of public taste is an old story. If sales are the sole aim, it is much easier to make a lot of money by exploiting people's basic human needs and weaknesses. To encourage the listener to think for himself is to risk splintering the market into numerous levels of demand and to make his buying habits unpredictable. It is no accident that one of the record industry's two top trade journals is called *Cash Box.* Sold primarily to record dealers, this magazine and its competitor, *Billboard,* also are widely read by disk jockeys, program directors, and others who handle recordings in broadcasting. The balance of their readership is suggested by a back section featuring juke boxes, pinball and merchandise (candy, etc.) and gambling slot machines. With half a million juke boxes collecting $250 million a year at the rate of 10 cents for three minutes of 45 r. p. m. music, this is more than a mere adjunct to the record industry.

Each week both *Billboard* and *Cash Box* publish tabulations of the best-selling LPs and 45 r. p. m. singles, supplemented with data on which new records are likely to break into the top 100 list, which records already on the list are likely to jump to higher positions, which records received the greatest amount of air time during the week, and much other information. A January 1964 issue of *Cash Box,* for example, would inform you that Elvis Presley's "Bossa Nova Baby," no longer in the American top 100, had moved up from sixth to third place among Japan's top ten and was in second and third place respectively in Denmark and Sweden. The nation's two thousand disk jockeys could turn to *Billboard's* "Ready-to-Go Programing" feature for a list of 20 "middle-road singles" culled from the Hot Hundred and listed in the same order but omitting such items as "Louie, Louie," "Surfin' Bird," and "The Nitty Gritty."

The Pop Music Spectrum Today

A survey of the top 100 LPs or of the disk jockey shows in any American city's radio stations would indicate a patterned spectrum of markets geared largely to different age groups. For the generation that was young in the days of Glenn Miller's swing, there have been memorial reissues of his recordings as well as "salutes" and "tributes" to this well-known bandleader. The latter, usually the product of obscure fly-by-night manufacturers, display Miller's name in large type on the record jacket, overshadowing the information that in this recording the tunes associated with the Miller band are being performed by another group. This is only one example of the many ways in which Tin Pan Alley's successors have far exceeded Charles K. Harris' dreams of exploitation in the field of popular music. Glenn Miller is not the only "name" bandleader to whom such money-making tributes have been devoted, nor have all those thus saluted been so conveniently deceased.

A more sugary sound, directed initially to the feet of 1930's dancing adults, has been produced with little variation for that generation by the bands of Wayne King, Sammy Kaye, Guy Lombardo, Lawrence Welk, and others. Welk and Kaye respectively summed up their efforts in the mottoes "rippling rhythm" and "swing and sway," while critics dubbed their fidelity to a bland formula as "ricky-ticky" music, referring to the metronomic monotony of their standardized beat. Few of these bands today are among the top 100 LPs, but they are well represented in the Schwann catalog of currently available long-playing records. Typical titles are "Enjoy Yourself" and "Midnight Serenade."

Appealing largely to the same age group are the newer orchestras of Mantovani, Melachrino, Paul Weston, André Kostelanetz, and David Rose, characterized by shimmering strings and slick arrangements of the show tunes of Victor Herbert, Cole Porter, Jerome Kern, and others, as well as film scores and "favorite waltzes" adapted as mood music for "easy listening" or as a background for dining and conversation. Typical of the genre are such album titles as "Music for Dreaming" and "Lure of Paradise."

For younger ears, the same romantic haze is frequently given a touch of torch by Roger Williams, Jackie Gleason, Percy Faith, and Billy Vaughn. Closely related to these instrumental mood stylists is an array of singers. Album titles are indicative: Joni James ("I'm Your Girl"), Peggy Lee ("Mink Jazz"), Julie London ("Latin in a Satin Mood"), Della Reese ("Della by Starlight"). The emphasis tends to be on sultry-voiced sexiness.

Male singers are somewhat harder to classify. The basic pop style began with Russ Columbo and Bing Crosby in the early thirties, who introduced a resonant crooning technique highly appropriate both to the relaxed syncopations of the swing bands and to the sentimental show tunes. In the forties Frank Sinatra created a new image of the crooner as a lovesick boy, which was copied with simpering effectiveness and carried in the direction of effeminacy by Mel Tormé and Vic Damone, with instrumental accompaniment palely reflecting the cool style of jazz. Later Sinatra began a new career as a mature singer with a more virile pose typified in the album title *Love Is a Kick*. Although the mantle of current popularity has been handed down from Crosby to Sinatra and more current favorites, the older singers have not been eclipsed by the new. They have held the generation to which they first appealed and added younger adherents as well. Perry Como, Nat "King" Cole, and others who never quite became the symbolic boyfriends of a generation nonetheless have held important places for two decades. Significantly, all have tended to move with the times; Sinatra's *Only the Lonely* and *All Alone* are paralleled by Cole's *Dear Lonely Hearts* and Andy Williams' *Lonely Street* albums.

Veering in the direction of jazz and in some cases overlapping with it are such groups as those of Dave Brubeck, George Shearing, Jonah Jones, and Cal Tjader, which appeal to today's college crowd on much the same terms as Benny Goodman, Artie Shaw, and other swing stars in the forties. To these commercialized cool-jazz ensembles must be added Miles Davis and other creative jazzmen who have become popular without going commercial and outright commercialists such as Al Hirt and Henry Mancini, who offer nothing but a clever formula of simulated jazz effects, performed with technical skill.

As a kind of subcategory there has long been a niche reserved for novelty songs appealing chiefly to high school youngsters. The Betty Boop of the 1930s was followed by the 1940s' "Mairzy Doats" and the hilarious parodies of Spike Jones. The 1950s introduced the nutty Chipmunks, Crazy Otto, and Ira Ironside ("Music for People with $3.98"). Current hits of 1964 include the Smothers Brothers' *Curb Your Tongue, Knave* and *Think Ethnic*.

The Biggest Category: Rock and Roll

Separate from the pop listings in *Cash Box* and *Billboard* are those records produced for the "country and western" and "rhythm and blues" markets. Over the years a few "country" singers such as Hank Williams and Jerry Lee Lewis have scored in the general market, but the biggest breakthroughs have involved rhythm and blues. As a market category, R&B has become a euphemism for the Negro ghetto, but properly speaking it refers to a style of popular music prevalent in the Southwest which harnessed a propulsive rhythm section to a funky shouted blues in a style that came to be known as rock and roll. As early as the 1940s, Louis Jordan and his Tympany Five popularized tunes like "Let the Good Times Roll" and provided the model for Woody Herman's novelty "Caldonia." But it was not until 1956 that the real impact came — not from a Negro R&B artist but from a white Mississippi boy, Elvis Presley. In the argot of the music industry, his style and that of some others — Jerry Lee Lewis, Johnny Cash, Carl Perkins — was called "rockabilly," essentially an adaptation of the hard-driving rhythmic blues by Southern country-and-western players, first discovered and promoted by Sam Phillips, owner of Sun Records in Memphis, Tenn.

There had been earlier crazes, as when bobby-soxed teen-agers mobbed the Paramount Theater in the 1940s to sigh and swoon for the young Frank Sinatra. But none approached the Presley smash. Five of the twelve top hits of 1956 were Presley items; in that one year he matched the score of the best-selling artists of the preceding decade and went on to surpass them. In the 15-year period 1948—1964, Presley, a late starter, has hit the number-one spot 17 times as compared with five times for Perry Como, his closest rival, who was recording throughout this period.

Teen-agers went wild over Presley, boosting the record industry's total sales volume by 45.8 percent in 1956 — from $227 million to $331 million, with a continuing upsurge the following year to $400 million. One of his songs, "You Ain't Nothin' but a Hound Dog," was taken directly from the funky blues, but most of the others lack its wry humor. "Heartbreak Hotel," "Love Me Tender," and other ballads are closer to the country-and-western style with their raw sentimentality. These are anguished whines of desperate desire, given a libidinous leaven with the borrowed blues rhythm. Whatever else may be said about him, Presley has consistently shown a rare talent for subtle voicings within his chosen idiom; he can turn instantly from tears to laughter and encompass bravado, gentleness, and sly humor in a single piece — all to the same steady, twanging beat. One of his hits, "All Shook Up," became a journalist's label for the juvenile delinquents of the time.

Since Presley's debut a host of imitators have kept rock and roll and its many variants dominant on the best-selling singles charts and account for a substantial segment of the top hundred LPs. The trend has incidentally widened the market for Negro rhythm-and-blues performers, including the quasi-jazz "soul" music of Ray Charles and others.

Pop Folk and the Beatles

In 1963 there was a significant upsurge of popularity for folk music and pseudo-folk music. For years, such singers as Burl Ives and the Weavers had been gaining a widening influence. More recently Bob Dylan, Joan Baez, Pete Seeger, the new Christy Minstrels, and Peter, Paul and Mary scored commercial successes. Rough-hewn traditional folk singers were followed by more polished stylists with clever arrangements and even newly written songs in folk style, culminating in highly commercialized "pop folk" ensembles like the Modern Folk Quartet, whose repertory contains only a smattering of traditional folksongs. Even this group has a certain freshness within the pop field, and among the commercial successes have been many songs of protest related to the struggle for racial equality — Pete Seeger's *We Shall Overcome* album (Columbia CL 2101)

49

eclipsed LPs by Sinatra and Nat Cole on the Top 100, and others generally less explicit placed even higher.

Some hailed this development as a breath of fresh air for pop music, but it jarred others who preferred a safer formula. In a letter published in *Broadcasting* in January 1964, O. J. Keller, president of WTAX in Springfield, Ill., hinted that it was time to clamp down on "message" songs as illicit editorializing, and he called upon broadcasting executives to intervene in their disk jockeys' programing.

The right formula was apparently found in the Beatles, an English group arising out of the "skiffle music" that has for some time served as a British counterpart to rock and roll, if it is not an actual offshoot. Their impact, triggered by promotional techniques that will be discussed in the next chapter, was the biggest to hit the pop music industry since Presley. Space does not permit a full assessment of their appeal. Michael Frayn in the London *Observer* has attributed much of it to sheer bland "niceness." Their stylistic range is minimal by comparison with Presley; they lack the tearful frenzy of many rock-and-roll stars, yet they preserve the twang and the steady beat, and a modest dollop of feigned emotion. In addition to other tunes, their repertory nods toward New Orleans jazz ("When the Saints Go Marching In") and folk ("My Bonnie"); one of their lesser hits is called "Roll Over, Beethoven." Like no other soloist or group, however, they have functioned as self-caricaturing personalities, eliciting a fantastic response to their looks and mannerisms. Whatever may be said of the Beatles as musical performers, their feature film *A Hard Day's Night* and interviews with the press reveal them as real and likable people capable of laughing at their own public personalities. This no doubt accounts for their endurance in the face of imitators such as the Rolling Stones and the Animals.

In addition to holding first, second, fourth, and three

other places on the Top 100 singles list, as well as first, second, and two other places among the Top 100 albums throughout early 1964, the Beatles sold 1.7 million copies of a single, "Can't Buy Me Love," in advance orders before release date and before purchasers had heard the song. This feat surpassed a previously unprecedented 1.5 million Presley advance sale. By the end of 1964, the Beatles had four million-selling singles and three "golden albums" — LPs selling at least $1,000,000 worth of copies at factory prices — and new entries riding high on the charts. A dozen records by other groups — among them "My Boyfriend Got a Beatle Haircut" and "We Love You Beatles" — quickly headed for the Top 100 soon after the Beatles' debut, to be followed by many more. There was even a bid for satire of an involuted kind; a group called the Bagels parodied the Beatles' top single in "I Want to Hold Your Hair."

These antics may qualify as harmless fun; certainly they are in a sense a fitting answer to Mr. Keller's indictment of "message" songs. Not only do they fill the industry's coffers, but they encourage citizens to echo a mindless "Yeah, yeah, yeah" instead of pondering the embarrassing questions embedded in Bob Dylan's "Blowin' In the Wind." "Soul" is all right when it is nothing more than an ethnic fetish as in Ray Charles' quasi-jazz *Ingredients in a Recipe for Soul;* it does not challenge the hit-making formula of "what's good is what sells." Given a choice between songs that promote maturity and those that cater to "mixed-up hearts," the latter make for a perennially more lucrative market. No song is without a message of some kind, and cash values can be rigged by calculated plugging that creates sales for what the promoter deems "good." But we must ask: "Good for whom and to what purpose?" What message is the pop music industry selling us with the songs they persuade us to listen to?

INSIDE POP MUSIC

The basic difference between jazz and popular music, as we have already seen, is a difference between creativity and commercialism. As André Hodeir has astutely demonstrated in his book *Jazz: Its Evolution and Essence,* the mere presence or absence of such features as swing, blues style, or improvisation does not certify a work as being jazz, though certainly they are important. Within the orbit of jazz it is possible to speak of stagnation, the failure of a musician to grow, develop, and enrich the evolving tradition, the tendency to lapse into clichés and repeat himself, or to become stultified in a style that has ceased to be original. This is true of any art — imagine a Stravinsky incapable of moving beyond *Petrushka* and spending a lifetime applying its techniques to other melodic sequences, or a Picasso doomed to a career of painting different subjects

52

in the exact style of *Les Demoiselles d'Avignon*. Granting the validity of the original, such repetition is the death of art.

When a creative artist ceases to be creative, this is tragic. But when he abandons creativity, listening to the sound of the cash register instead of his artistic intuition, he has gone commercial. There is yet a further step: the musician who has nothing of his own to say but has found it lucrative to imitate the real thing or even to concoct a product that has no relationship to art and no reason for being except its market value. The swing sound of a Ray Anthony, for example, may be pleasant, but it is only a replica of the big band swing of the 1940s. It owes much to jazz, but it has nothing of its own with which to honor the debt — its whole substance is a tissue of jazz clichés from which creativity has been drained. It is predigested and bite-sized, offering the listener really very little to listen to and certainly nothing to wrestle with or be moved by.

Let us be quite clear that these are not hard and fast terms. There is creativity within the pop music field — obvious examples are the wit of Cole Porter and the phenomenal dramatic gift of Barbra Streisand as a singer who, in her field, rivals the jazz singer Billie Holiday. But as a genre, pop music does not require creativity to succeed. What is asked rather is technical proficiency. Compare the two trumpeters, Miles Davis and Al Hirt. As a creative artist, Davis must bring something new and personal to each performance; everything depends on what he has to say on his instrument. There may be half a dozen different Miles Davis interpretations of "Round About Midnight," reflecting Davis' growth or decline over the years. Hirt, by contrast, need only apply his skill as a player to a stock arrangement of "Java" to make an ephemeral hit. After the hit's novelty is expended, it is discarded

53

like a paper cup; having exhausted its sales potential, it has served its purpose. Like novelty toys, souvenirs, or bric-a-brac, it is an assembly-line product designed to catch the ear and sell fast, not to endure. Hence the performance itself is only concerned with surface tricks, however skillful and deft these may be.

The Making of a Pop Music Star

The psychologist, T. W. Adorno, well known for his pioneer study *The Authoritarian Personality*, observed as long ago as 1941 that "the fundamental characteristic of popular music [is] standardization." [1] Not only the form but the details are stock items which are "hidden behind a veneer of individual 'effects' whose prescriptions are handled as the experts' secret, however open the secret may be to musicians generally." [2] This general principle applies not only to the music but to the public image of the star performer.

Louis Weertz was born in Omaha and reared in Des Moines, the son of a Lutheran pastor and a former music teacher. By the age of three he could play the piano by ear, and at eight he was putting on a one-boy show at church socials. In high school he was director of the orchestra and choir. After serving in the Navy in World War II, he continued his studies and began appearing in concerts throughout the Midwest. In 1952 he moved to New York and enrolled at the Juilliard School of Music, where one of his instructors was jazz pianist Teddy Wilson. After Juilliard he continued his studies in this idiom with Lennie Tristano, while earning a living by playing in cocktail lounges.

It was during this period that young Weertz was "discovered" by Arthur Godfrey's Talent Scouts, and soon afterward he recorded his first LP — *The Boy Next Door*. By this time he had changed his name to Roger Williams.

Now, a decade later, he is the world's leading pop pianist. Over seven million LPs bearing his adopted name have been sold.

The change of name is symptomatic. In jazz, a name like Beiderbecke or Thelonious Monk is no handicap. But in pop music, as in Hollywood, good publicity means conformity with a preconceived image. Any talented American born with a German or Russian name, for example, is almost certain to be painted over with an English one, since this is the only sure way to avoid the effects of prejudice. But not just any name will do, and even English ones that are ungainly may be exchanged for those that have an appropriate sound.

The "boy next door" image has stuck with Roger Williams throughout his rapid rise to stardom. Eight of the ten photos of Williams that have been used on his record jackets show him full-face with a gentle, ingratiating smile. The other two show him at the piano. Whatever his range of expression as a person offstage, the winsome smile of the "boy next door" covers the major part of his public image, which is dovetailed with such album titles as these: *Daydreams, Roger Williams Invites You to Dance, Near You, Always, For You.* The image is consistently decorous, reassuring rather than heady or exuberant. These attributes in turn may support an equally stereotyped image of another performer — Julie London is always sultry. Williams' piano style and repertory is likewise standardized. The word "fabulous" is the exhilarant rubric of ten LPs such as *Songs of the Fabulous Forties.*

What is fabulous about the 1940s, 1950s, 1960s or "the fabulous century" is suggested in another album title: "It's a Big, Wide, Wonderful World." What makes it so is the pastor's son from next door, who is such a decent fellow. With his doctorate in music and his dabbling in jazz, he has technique to spare in his cocktail-lounge renditions of such gems as "Tico Tico," "Autumn Leaves," "Nature Boy," and "Zip-a-Dee-Doo-Dah" — "melodies that will live forever," thanks to nimble fingers and rippling arpeggios. To complete the image are albums in which *Roger Williams Plays Beautiful Waltzes* and *Roger Williams Plays Gershwin Rhapsody in Blue.* The latter, along with Addinsell's *Warsaw Concerto,* are the nearest he has come to the classical orbit — works that seem "classical" only to those who find "Nature Boy" worth going back for.

Not all of Williams' repertory is equally banal; it includes an occasional standard like "I Got Rhythm," but these are rare within an abundance of trivia. Significantly, "My Reverie" is included — the Tin Pan Alley adaptation rather than Debussy's original piano piece. But in pop music, the tune is secondary; "Donkey Serenade" and "I'm Always Chasing Rainbows" have in common with all the other "fabulous" Williams hits a certain blandness and pliancy to which his talents can add a bit of elegant froth. The formula has proved successful in sales; Williams' 10th-anniversary album is appropriately titled *The Solid Gold Steinway.* Having in hand a predictable commodity, any venture of creative growth would be tantamount to financial suicide.

Exploiting the Mass Market

Apologists and publicists for the pop music industry frequently retort to criticisms by saying that "this is what the public wants to hear." Unlike the implicit standards of art, the doctrine of "entertainment" is little more than a smokescreen to avoid responsibility and justify making money. No gimmick can be too contrived or phony, so long as it "entertains" — but in fact the real criterion is not "fun" for the listener; this is distinctly secondary to the industry's cash income.

Part of the entertainment doctrine holds that pop music is basically democratic; it simply fills the demands of the masses. When a politician takes such a stance, we call it demagogy, for there is no such thing as "meeting people where they are" en masse; people may be appealed to on various levels, challenging their highest potential for growth or playing on their insecurities and fears. At the very least, millions of listeners are led to settle for the pseudo-jazz of Ray Anthony or Al Hirt, thwarting their confrontation with the real thing, and the pianistic prettiness of Roger Williams inoculates them against the rigors of Serkin or Horowitz.

But the debasement of taste goes much further. There seems to be something akin to Gresham's law operating in the pop music industry, whereby bad music drives out the good. It is not that listeners are stupid but that song promoters find it easier and more remunerative to flood the market with wave after wave of ersatz and froth. Trashy music is easier to produce in large volume, wears out quickly and, once the demand is stimulated, can readily be replaced with a newer model. The teen-age segment of the mass market is the most vulnerable in this respect, and it is a gold mine for the industry, accounting for the overwhelming bulk of hit singles and a substantial share of LPs.

The teens are formative years, the period of learning and groping toward maturity. After puberty boys and girls are no longer dependent children, yet they are unprepared for adulthood. Throughout high school, especially, they are increasingly aware of being on the threshold of independence. Acceptance and status within their group are very important, and great seriousness mingles with extreme enthusiasms of brief duration. Strong sexual ambivalences are set in motion — a teen-age girl wants to be sought after by all the boys (or at least the attractive ones) and to be both accepted and envied by all the girls. She wants to be loved — and also to love, to be in love, though she is somewhat afraid of the latter because this involves risk and possible heartache. And the teen-age boy, in his separate boy's world, undergoes his own counterpart of her struggle. He wants to be a man among men and also, hesitant to admit it to anyone but himself, to find love with the right girl. It is a time of abundant fantasy and idealism in which boys and girls alike entertain romantic illusions about themselves and each other, and about not only their own world but the adult world they will soon enter.

Literature, music and entertainment cannot ignore the teen-ager's needs. Only the most arid puritanism would think of banning adventure stories, mystery thrillers, romances or most of the inane fads to which teen-agers are prone. Whatever their role in adult life, these are part of adolescence. It is not fair to expect teen-age pop ballads, for example, to be full of mature wisdom and free of fantasy and sentiment. At the same time, however, the adult world cannot shirk its measure of responsibility in molding and guiding adolescent trends toward maturity. Here the doctrine of entertainment becomes pernicious as a cloak for the manipulation of volatile emotions and the inculcation of distorted values.

Healthy and Neurotic Fantasy

There is nothing inherently wrong in the fact that pop ballads tend to indulge in fantasy. For the teen-ager especially they thus serve as a vehicle for a normal, healthy process. According to the psychoanalyst Paul Lussheimer, daydreaming is a blend of realistic, logical thinking and unconscious, emotionally directed thinking. For the child it is a preventive against neurosis and, says Lussheimer, "even more in adolescence the daydream has significance not only as a healing agent against disappointments and frustrations but also as a medium for planning and healthy character formation." [3] In listening to the lyrics of a popular song, the teen-ager identifies himself with a character or viewpoint in the song and through fantasy repetition applies this new identity to his own situation, interpreting and revising it so as to overcome emotional dissatisfactions. This process is by no means limited to the pop song; its essentials were outlined by Aristotle in his theory of *katharsis* as the emotional release produced in the audience by classic Greek tragedy. Primarily, according to Lussheimer, daydreams arise from anxiety. They do not solve problems, but they provide relief from stress.

The form which normal daydreaming takes is not far removed from the visual and verbal language of everyday life. The daydreamer may thus escape momentarily from a frustrating situation, but he escapes into another situation that is still located in the world as he knows it. A romantic pop ballad couched in terms close to the adolescent's own experience (or the adult's, for that matter) can therefore fulfill both his reality and fantasy needs. The more deeply rooted it is in an authentic view of human relationships, of course, the more helpful it will be in structuring his thinking, provided it also includes fantasy elements that makes it accessible.

There is firm support in both Christian doctrine and tradition for these clinical observations. Consider the spiritual refreshment to be found in the Song of Solomon or in the poetry of Gerard Manley Hopkins:

> *Glory be to God for dappled things —*
> *For skies of couple-colour as a brinded cow;*
> *For rose-moles all in stipple upon trout that swim . . .*

There is rich fantasy here and a buoyant reveling in the beauty of God's creation. Pop ballads may seldom mention God, and none that I know is a match for Hopkins or other great poets, but there is the same kind of exuberance in the lyrics of Cole Porter's "I Love You." There is nothing cloying or gross about them; they express beautifully the feeling of being in love. Love, he is saying, transforms the lover's world; he cannot contain his emotions, and it is as if everything in creation mirrors his joyous mood. It is pure fantasy: winds and hills do not really say "I love you," as they do in the song; and in fact love itself is more than sentimental exuberance. But the link with reality is secure; what grim sobersides would deny that love does — and should — affect people in this way? With such lyrics, why not — in the words of another pop standard — let yourself go? The best pop songs all have something of this quality of sentimental daydreaming or fantasy. It need not always be happy to be healthy. Consider Hoagy Carmichael's "Stardust," a classic of nostalgic fantasy. If you study its lyrics, you will note certain checks and balances: "sometimes" — it is not an obsession with the past; "I wonder why" — a note of musing whereby the sad lover detaches himself from his nostalgia; "but that was long ago" — it is recognized as being past. Granted the song's basic sentimentality, it is a legitimate fantasy of savoring past joys. In Lussheimer's terms, it provides resilience against the anxiety implicit in "the lonely night" of lost love. Tension is resolved in the recapturing of the old *tendresse* — the image presented is a partial reworking of an undoubtedly more bittersweet reality, and the important new reality is the dating element which expresses an acceptance of the fact that the relationship is over.

Song after song could be analyzed in similar fashion to show how, within the pop idiom and with no apparent jazz or other influences, it is possible to express a wide range of emotion — from "Happy Days Are Here Again" to "When Your Lover Has Gone" — in terms that are basically honest and healthy, terms that, however fantasied, retain contact with reality.

But as Lussheimer shows, there is also such a thing as neurotic daydreaming — not merely a temporary relief from anxiety that may aid in overcoming frustrations, but an escape from reality itself or a distortion of it so basic that it can only increase frustration. Neurotic daydreaming is compulsive and debilitating; rather than seeking elements of reality in a fantasy situation, it expends great emotional energy to sustain a precarious denial of reality. A separate fantasy world like that of the schizophrenic becomes a substitute for reality, a wishful substitute world in which problems are magically solved. "It acts like a drug," says Lussheimer, "and the habit formation becomes stronger and stronger." [4] The fantasied self-image that takes part in the pseudosolution is not the person's everyday self, but what Karen Horney calls the neurotic "idealized image" — Walter Mitty in shining armor or the invalid as an Olympic track star. Hence the neurotic derives no benefit from daydreaming, since it leads only to the imaginary resolution of his inner conflicts. Contact with reality only defeats him once more, sending him back to consoling fantasy.

Passivity, fatalism, and tearful pathos are predominant characteristics of the typical rock-and-roll ballad, along with a kind of magical dependence exactly like that of neurotic fantasy. If we were to summarize the worldview expressed in this type of song, we would find that it looks somewhat like this:

1. Things happen to me. I have no control over them and no responsibility for them.

2. Life has no discernible meaning or purpose; it is governed by an inscrutable fate: "What will be, will be."

3. I am alone in this frightening, incomprehensible world. (Although there is safety in conforming with the crowd, this doesn't alleviate my basic insecurity.)

4. If love were to happen to me — *your* love — all my anxieties would be magically resolved. You, the love object, are so incomparably wonderful (in fact, divine) that I worship you and would do virtually anything to obtain you.

5. If you withhold your love, or if, as fate might decree, you turn it off and give it to someone else, my loneliness and anxiety become unbearable.

This is a worldview that is relevant to the human condition and especially to urban mass society, reflecting man's lostness and need for meaningfulness. It is not concocted out of thin air. But it is a highly distorted view which, instead of breaking through to a higher truth or a deeper reality, attempts a solution within the confines of its own brokenness by a vain process of imaginary healing. Perhaps the pivotal flaw is a misunderstanding of the nature of the self and of love. In reality man must accept both his own limitedness and that of others if he is to find relevant meaning which transcends and encompasses the limits of the human predicament. The love which he needs is the love of God in Christ, which can liberate him for that mutual sharing of integrity which is human love between man and woman. In this human love under God, sexual fulfillment is not unimportant but it is set in a context in which its "magic" is only metaphorical, one among many of the joys of life, not the demonic salvation of neurotic fantasy. Like all real sacrilege, the attempt to worship one's own idealized image or its projection in a fantasied love object is doomed to fail not because God is peevish but because such an attempt runs counter to reality. Any human being who becomes an idol is bound to disappoint the idolizer's expectations and cause his fantasy to come apart at the seams.

Today's pop ballads seldom are more frankly sexual in their language than those of earlier decades, but they are often more suggestive because of the emphasis on sexual-erotic gratification. Such clichés as "your loving charms" or the assertion of one's incapacity to resist them, the frantic ardor with which the words "I want to hold your hand" are uttered by the Beatles and others, the frequent occurence of such themes as the "prisoner of love" or of desire — all of these narrow the sexual relationship to a hungry craving. Possibly the stated aims — let me kiss you, hold your hand, know that you care — are euphemisms for more complete sexual experience. Or it may be that, as in Victorian times, holding the loved one's hand is itself raised to the level of an orgasmic event. (The ecstasy of teen-agers who have succeeded in merely seeing a pop singing star face to face is a case in point, reminiscent of Hindu *darsana,* whereby the devotee acquires merit by being in the presence of a holy man.) In either case, love is reduced to the single dimension of desire — a desire with frequent overtones of simple neurosis and even such pathological conditions as masochism. Once in a while the demand is for ordinary human "love and understanding," but more typically the terms are those of a sexual mystique involving not two persons but only a self and his or her object of desire. Real personal attributes of character, mind, spirit, or conscience rarely occur. The object of desire is not depicted as witty, warmhearted, or anything else humanly transcending sexuality — though in real love these qualities are important. What we get instead, usually, is a catalog of "what you do to me"; the lover (more accurately the craver) has nothing to offer but adulation — the adulation not of a man but of a high-strung set of reflexes, quivering with anticipations of ecstasy and offering his object of desire fantastic rewards — the moon, the stars, his own soul — in exchange for the gratification he seeks.

The basic theme of the neurotic ballad has many variants — jealousy and heartache rank high among them, and loneliness figures not only as an undoubted underlying motive but also as an explicit statement. Even when the self is not voicing erotic desire, he is still expressing what Martin Buber calls an "I-it" relationship which, when boiled

63

down to its essence, says: "I want to use you" — sexually, emotionally, or in some other way — instead of "I value you for yourself." This is true, for example, when the self assumes a he-man pose instead of the groveling one. When Elvis Presley sings "It's Now Or Never" (to the tune of the traditional Italian favorite, "O Sole Mio"), he makes it clear that the romance is over if his beloved does not yield to his frantic entreaty.

The Fabrication of Atmosphere and Mood

Whatever the literary limits of such pop standards as "I Love You" and "Stardust," the typical rock-and-roll ballad of today represents a sharp decline into banality. To read the lyrics in print, separate from the sounds that go with them, is almost embarrassing; they are so trite, so cliché-ridden, so lacking in even the most rudimentary literary taste and so raw in their statement — "please be mine," "kiss me," "don't leave me," etc. They lack not only depth but subtlety, and when they resort to metaphor it is generally from a stock of the obvious and well-worn.

Some years ago, Mitch Miller asserted that people only "half-listen" to pop songs. If the words get through, it is not by profound meditation but by massive repetition and by seepage through the general impact of sound in which they are delivered. For together with the impoverishment of pop song lyrics has gone a preoccupation with performance technique. Douglas Moore has observed that the modern pop ballad generally is not so much a song as a dance with words added. This is certainly true of every swing number, and much more so in rock and roll, where the listener's attention is drawn to the beat rather than to the lyric-carrying melody. Little can be said about the Beatles' "I Want to Hold Your Hand," for example, without actually hearing how the words are supported by trap drums and three electric guitars — and how on the word "hand," the vocal parts suddenly shift from unison to a frenzied harmonic dissonance that invests the word, and the line which it ends, with exaggerated emotional impact.

But this is only a specific case in a development that embraces far more than the Beatles or rock and roll. Since the early radio crooners — Rudy Vallee, Russ Columbo, and Bing Crosby — pop vocalists have moved from mere singers to "song stylists." The initial impetus was the personal expressiveness we find in the blues, but in pop music it became standardized as an artificial device cultivated for effect and applied to formula ballads that had no special meaning for the singer. Sedulous ingenuity is lavished on the cultivation of a whimpering, choked-up delivery of songs like "Forget Him," which contains heartbreak lyrics — but a singer with this style can transform a ballad like "There, I've Said It Again" into tortured misery (as Bobby Vinton does) simply by the tremolo effect he gives to its bland words. There is a difference between the pop artistry of a Barbra Streisand, with her dramatization of carefully chosen ballads — mostly of pre-1950 vintage — and the more widespread exploitation of second-rate musical materials for sheer effect. It is the latter which is the main trend; if carried to its logical conclusion the result would be no longer music but a mere pastiche of sound effects.

What is true of vocal styling is equally true of instrumental playing. The massing of strings into shimmering glissandos without any intrinsic musical value to produce an alluring emotional aura is only one of numerous effects that are used. Stock sound effects such as rippling waves may also be heard, and the use of the echo chamber coupled with amplification tricks can take the husky boudoir voice of the skilled vocal stylist and make of it an erotic aural fantasy totally eclipsing anything human.

What is wrong with this? Primarily it educates the listener away from reality and toward fantasy in somewhat the same way that the resourceful and talented prostitute pampers her customer and thereby places him at a loss to experience sex in a relationship of mutual love with its ups and downs. As T. W. Adorno wrote in 1941, before pop music had gone very far in this direction:

> *Structural standardization aims at standard reactions. Listening to popular music is manipulated not only by its promoters but, as it were, by the inherent nature of this music itself, into a system of response-mechanisms wholly antagonistic to the ideal of individuality in a free, liberal society.*[5]

The manipulative character of pop music has grown and proliferated since then. Ten years ago, Harvey Swados called the pop music industry

> *a vast apparatus devoted to the manufacturing of public taste and to the conditioning of that taste through constant reiteration (the disk jockey and the juke box) which creates a mass demand for mediocrity and worse.*[6]

Beatlemania

The desire for junk is stimulated, wrote Swados, through "carefully calculated campaigns of saturation." An excellent example of this may be found in the astute promotion of the Beatles, an obscure Liverpool rock-and-roll quartet, to a position of international fame in 1963 to 1964. The Beatles were formed in 1959 and "discovered" in October 1961 by Brian Epstein, who became their manager and built up a following for them through judicious bookings, working up from small cabarets to ballrooms, theaters, and the concert stage, while issuing a steady stream of publicity. Their first record release in the United States, early in 1963, did not sell. By October 1963, however, they had reached national prominence in Britain, and this fact was used as the basis of a publicity buildup in the

66

United States, including an 8-page feature in *Life*. Capitol Records rushed its new Beatles releases ahead of schedule to cash in on the publicity and sent out a million copies of a 4-page booster tabloid to disk jockeys, the press, and dealers. It also supplied disk jockeys with an ingenious recording and a script. The script contained questions for the disk jockey to ask; the recording consisted of answers to these questions spoken by the Beatles, creating the illusion of an exclusive interview — a gimmick strongly appealing to the disk jockey's vanity. This, more than anything else, stimulated record sales, which in turn led to increased radio play. By the time the Beatles appeared on the Ed Sullivan TV show, they were already a sensation.

According to some reports, the publicity men took no chances when the Beatles first arrived in the United States. The New York Times asserted: "One girl said that several friends had been offered tickets to see the Beatles and $5 each to go in and 'make like you're crazy.'" This, of course, was heatedly denied by the head of the Beatles' team of 18 press agents.

At the time of their American debut, the Beatles had slipped from first to tenth place on the best-selling singles chart in Great Britain. The success in the United States boosted their popularity in their own country once again, in addition to selling more than 3,000,000 copies of "I Want to Hold Your Hand" and nearly 2,000,000 copies of their second post-debut single, "She Loves You." LP sales skyrocketed similarly, and *Cash Box* reported that sales of Beatles toys, dolls, clothing, and other products were expected to total $50,000,000 by the end of the year.

Crazes of the proportions of "Beatlemania" do not occur every year, but the manipulated popularity they achieved is only an extraordinary example of the everyday occurrence. If pop singers or groups can reach a certain level of popularity, they are virtually assured a further boost by disk jockeys and by the average teen-ager's tendency to conform. In the case of the Beatles craze, many records scored sales simply because of the Beatles' success. Epic Records issued a huge broadsheet during the Beatles' American debut, capitalizing on the fact that Dave Clark had "beat the Beatles," taking first place on the British sales charts. Soon afterward his hit single, "Glad All Over," entered the *Cash Box* Top 100, jumping quickly from No. 71 to No. 43 and still climing in its third week. Simultaneously such songs as "My Boyfriend Got a Beatle Haircut" and "Beatle Crazy" appeared respectively in *Cash Box's* "Looking Ahead" and "Newcomer Picks" features.

Pop Music and Social Popularity

The social psychologist David Riesman, author of *The Lonely Crowd,* says that the tastes of teen-age pop music listeners are undiscriminating. In contrast to those of the same age group who listen to jazz and tend to develop "strict and often highly articulate standards for judging jazz," pop music fans whom he interviewed seldom got beyond the categories of "swell" or "lousy." How do they decide which is "swell"? A typical answer by a 17-year-old girl was: "If it's popular, we go for it; if it's played on the Hit Parade."

The range of influences stemming from this naive conformity and uncritical acceptance of whatever the music industry produces is considerable, according to Riesman.

> *The functions of music for this group are* social — *the music gives them something to talk or kid about with friends; an opportunity for competitiveness in judging which tunes will become hits, coupled with a lack of concern about how hits are actually made; an opportunity for identification with star singers or bandleaders as "personalities"* . . .[7]

Conformity to group preferences, moreover, tends to be

internalized and functions even when the individual teen-ager is alone. Radio and television keep the listener in step:

> *It is the pressure of conformity with the group that invites and compels the individual to have recourse to the media both in order to learn from them what the group expects and to identify with the group by sharing a common focus for attention and talk.*[8]

In addition to the shaping of teen-age attitudes and values through the production and promotion of songs, the world of pop music exerts its influence through various satellite industries such as fan clubs, suppliers of photos of star singers, and magazines like *Hit Parader* and *Sixteen*. The former, founded in 1941, publishes texts of hit songs, but this nowadays is largely a mopping-up operation; by the time the magazine reaches its readers the songs have burned themselves out. For example, 21 of the 22 hits given in the February 1964 *Hit Parader* were on the December 28, 1963, *Cash Box* scoreboard; only 11 of these were still on it by January 25, and by February 22 only one was left and it was in 65th place. Other features include record reviews of LPs, articles and gossip about song stylists, and brief, generally good coverage of jazz and folk music. By no means sedate or wholly conformist, *Hit Parader* in its editorials not only celebrates "the mighty world of entertainment" but has saluted performers for acts of social responsibility such as participation in the March On Washington and spot radio announcements against school dropouts. At the same time, it is instructive to note how the fantasy world of "entertainment" proliferates. The same company, Charlton Publications, issues *Hit Parader* and also *Rock and Roll Songs* for the Negro market, as well as the "girlie" magazines for men, *Caper* and *Escapade,* featuring nude glamour photos and other material perpetuating a narrow erotic view of sex compatible with the typical pop song lyrics on the "adult" level.

Sixteen, a newer magazine launched in 1960, tends to be much more sensational and spectacular than *Hit Parader,* with gossip and glamour photos of pop singers and movie idols predominating. A typical issue is liberally sprinkled with house advertisements for prize contests, "autographed" star photos and candids, "tremendous color pinups" and life stories, a "Secret Star Address Book of All the Top Teen Idols," a "beauty book" for girls, a membership club which publishes the names of those who join if they request it, and a fantastic offer inviting the reader to submit his "secret dream." "No matter what it is that you secretly long for, write it down." "*16* is going to stop at nothing to get just what you want." Apparently it is inconceivable to the editors that their readers could want anything outside the range of the star cult. Their suggestions are "a truly personal keepsake from your dream guy," the opportunity to be photographed with a star, or to write him a letter and maybe even get a personal answer.

In *Sixteen,* best-selling song stylist Connie Francis ("Rock 'N Roll Million Sellers," "Award Winning Motion Picture Hits," etc.) conducts a full-page column, "Your Secret Sister," answering letters from teen-age girls. She gives advice on how to make a boy jealous, how to prepare for a modeling career, what gifts to give a boyfriend, and, in effect, what is the next best thing to actually meeting a singing star: join his fan club and, if he visits Kansas City (the girl's home town), "you can be by the stage door when he comes in or out."

This, it would seem, summarizes the fantasy life which is fabricated for today's teen-agers under the doctrine of entertainment. Such things never actually reach their full culmination — there is a point at which teen-agers are forced to mature or at which parents arise to protest the encroachment of the industry on younger children. Nevertheless, the pervasive influence of commercialism and the exploitation of emotions along neurotic, debilitating lines take their toll, especially among those who lack countervailing resources. In a society in which one out of every three marriages ends in divorce and many others are held together by little more than conventional taboos, each generation is more vulnerable than the last and readier to accept unquestioningly the idolatrous and hedonistic values that helped to unfit their estranged parents for a healthy, mature relationship. Given free rein, perhaps the pop music industry will have our grandchildren so thoroughly "entertained" that they will forgo mature love and cry themselves to sleep each night to the tune of completely dehumanized electronic sound effects in view of a floor-to-ceiling fluorescent color photo, double life-size, of their erotic idol, to whom they may write from time to time for synthetic assurance of passionate desire.

But before matters come to that, it is encouraging to note that there is still a market for healthy commercial music — both pop standards and the occasional healthy new hit — and still room for the creative voices of folk music and jazz with their traditions of protest and prophecy.

4

CREATIVE CURRENTS
IN TODAY'S JAZZ

Even at its best, pop music is limited to a sentimental view of life, usually focused narrowly on boy-girl relationships. Whatever might be the commercial value of songs expressing conscience or social responsibility, they would represent a departure from "entertainment" that is hardly to be expected from the music industry's tastemakers. Likewise, the relationship between pop and classical idioms has been consistently exploitative, involving raids on the concert hall for melodies on which to base sentimental ballads like "Full Moon and Empty Arms" (Rachmaninoff) and "Till the End of Time" (Chopin). Virtually by definition, commercial music does not lend itself to serious purposes beyond creating atmosphere in motion-picture sound tracks, where the burden of meaning is carried by the visual image and the spoken word.

There are many ways, however, in which jazz has demonstrated a creativity and depth that both express and transcend its norms and traditions. In addition to musically significant works, Duke Ellington has addressed himself to social problems with such compositions as "Nonviolent Integration" for orchestra (*The Symphonic Ellington*, Reprise 6097) and "King Fit the Battle of Alabam," an adaptation of the spiritual "Joshua" complete with text referring to freedom riders and the struggle of nonviolent church people against police dogs and fire hoses. Art Blakey contributes a hard bop interpretation of the struggle on *The Freedom Rider* (Blue Note 4156).

White jazz guitarist Charlie Byrd has improvised an extended fantasia on the protest song "Which Side Are You On," covering a whole LP side of his *Charlie Byrd at the Village Vanguard* (Offbeat 3008). Bop drummer Max Roach enlisted Coleman Hawkins, Nigerian drummer Olatunji and others in a boldly conceived *Freedom Now Suite* (Candid 8002), featuring jazz singer Abbey Lincoln. One side evokes the Negro's experience of slavery and emancipation; the other is divided between a salute to the emerging new African nations and a searing jazz lament over South African apartheid, "Tears for Johannesburg," which communicates eloquently in instrumental terms.

Perhaps the most productive in this area has been Charles Mingus, whose full-length LP work *The Black Saint and the Sinner Lady* (Impulse 35) is at once a sensitive personal statement about love and an impassioned expression of social struggle. Thoroughly jazz, its musical content ranges from languid classical style piano to hard-swinging dissonant ensemble sequences punctuated with gospel-shouting horns. One of its six tracks is subtitled "Stop! Look! And Sing Songs of Revolution!" Among Mingus' other, shorter works in this vein, scattered on several LPs, are "Fables of Faubus" (Candid 8005) and

"Freedom" (United Artists 14024), both hard-hitting vocals against Jim Crow, the moving instrumental "Prayer for Passive Resistance" (Mercury 20627), and the half-comical "O Lord, Don't Let Them Drop That Atomic Bomb on Me."

In addition to issuing such musical affirmations as these, both Negro and white jazzmen — Dizzy Gillespie, Cannonball Adderley, Gerry Mulligan, Randy Weston, and Clark Terry, to name only a few — have repeatedly given benefit concerts to raise funds for the Southern Christian Leadership Conference and other cause organizations. One of Charles Mingus' most consistently creative jazz concerts was a "Freedom Now" benefit performed by his sextet at Town Hall on April 4, 1964, for the Metropolitan Area NAACP Youth Council. A particularly striking example of this kind of dedication was the gesture of singer Joe Wiliams at a lawn concert at the home of Jackie Robinson on June 23, 1963. Williams had worked the night before in Chicago and arrived at Robinson's Stanford, Conn., home without having had any sleep. Last on the program, he waited patiently for four hours, closed the show with a highly emotional rendition of the Lord's Prayer — and also conributed $500 over and above his expenses in making the sleepless trip.

Although jazzmen have tended to confine their actions to the musical scene, when Count Basie happened to be in Tallahassee to play at a fraternity dance in December 1963, he joined a picket line of the Congress of Racial Equality that was protesting segregation at a nearby restaurant. Others have expressed their stand in a variety of ways ranging from the signing of petitions to the act of blind singer Al Hibbler, who went to Birmingham during the peak of the May 1963 campaign — the only Negro the police there refused to arrest.

All of these facts attest to a firm linkage between the

creativity of these men as artists and their integrity as persons. In a society of cash values in which many people are tempted to sell out and "go commercial" in their various walks of life, we find some jazzmen insisting on being themselves, enduring somehow on their own terms and even sticking their necks out to affirm their convictions. This hardly tallies with the lurid view of jazz often peddled by slick journalists, depicting jazz as originating in whorehouses, flourishing in speakeasies, and played today by narcotics addicts in night clubs.

How Jazzmen Feel About Night Clubs

The true picture includes some of these elements, but it is much more complex. Buddy Bolden was a regular church member; he and other jazzmen played in Storyville, but few of them played in its brothels. Charlie Parker and others of his generation underwent an agonized struggle with drug addiction; many jazzmen did not. It is true that jazz has tended to be associated with night clubs or dance halls, though it has also made its way into the concert hall. The fact is that the public has usually tended to think of jazzmen as entertainers and nothing more, while actually the full range of jazz includes this function but goes far beyond it. Charles Mingus, Don Friedman, and others have frequently stated that they would greatly prefer not to have to play in night clubs — largely because drinking and chatting patrons do not make the best audiences. Another reason is the programing. A recent evening at Birdland, "jazz corner of the world," alternated the fine creative talents of John Coltrane in his prime with the serviceable but undistinguished hard bop of Les McCann and the downright vulgar commercialism of Irene Reid, whose major contribution was a raunchy exploitation of sex. The juxtaposition was as incongruous and offensive as would be a program pairing Jascha Heifetz and Belle Barth. I suspect that some sort of Gresham's Law works against the creative artist in such situations, since it weights the audience in favor of the more vulgar and less creative.

Dizzy Gillespie, on the other hand, argues that the relaxed night-club atmosphere makes for better rapport, but he concedes: "There's a place for both clubs and concerts." Cannonball Adderley thinks the answer might lie in theaters. But the point is that night clubs, the silly jive talk of disk jockeys, the promotion and distribution of jazz records, and many other things are features of the commercial world of entertainment which impinge on jazzmen without their having much to say about it. Significantly, a man like Mingus will not hesitate to perform a piece like "Fables of Faubus" with its vocal references to the Ku Klux Klan despite the fact that night-club patrons expect only entertainment.

In recent years there have been attempts to create new settings in which jazz might be heard — in museums, at festivals such as the Newport Jazz Festival, in coffee houses, and in places like the Jazz Gallery, an unsuccessful New York experiment which provided a relaxed atmosphere and two types of seating arrangements: tables at which drinks were served and a general-admission section for those who just wanted to listen.

Jazz and the Concert Hall

The concert hall, however, has significance not only as a setting for jazz but as a meeting place between jazz and classical music. The interplay between the two dates back to the origins of jazz itself. At the height of his career, ragtime composer Scott Joplin wrote an opera, *Treemonisha*, published in 1911 but never staged, and a symphony announced to the press in 1916 but never performed. It was left to a classical composer, Igor Stravinsky, to write a *Ragtime for Eleven Instruments*

(Columbia ML 5772) in 1918 after studying Joplin's and others' piano works. "Jazz . . . has exerted a time-to-time influence on my music since 1918," he stated recently, "and blues and boogie-woogie occur in some of my most serious pieces." [1] The American composer Aaron Copland has written a set of *Four Piano Blues*. Darius Milhaud, after a visit to Harlem, returned to Paris in 1923 to write his "Negro ballet," *La Création du Monde*, the scoring of which bears closer resemblances to early jazz than George Gershwin's neo-Lisztian *Rhapsody in Blue*, written the following year. The work of many other European and American composers shows that jazz reached them and had its effect in both subtle and explicit ways. Even in the USSR, when Dmitri Shostakovich repudiated a number of his compositions as "decadent" in response to the cultural purge of 1936, his *Suite for Jazz Orchestra* (1934, unpublished MS) was not among them.

The Shostakovich suite is significant because it is one of the first attempts by a classical composer to write not only in jazz idiom but for jazz instruments. In 1945, Stravinsky went further, writing his *Ebony Concerto* for a specific jazz group, the Woody Herman Orchestra (Columbia ML 4398), but attempting to fuse both jazz and classical elements in its musical content. In the 1950s, Rolf Liebermann's *Concerto for Jazz Band and Orchestra* had a brief vogue. Most critics considered both the Stravinsky and Liebermann works interesting but unsuccessful experiments.

Since 1927, Duke Ellington has written a number of significant works in extended form, achieving a complexity and depth of expression within the jazz idiom that parallels the work of classical composers. Among them are *A Tone Parallel to Harlem, Liberian Suite, Black and Tan Fantasy,* and *Black, Brown, and Beige*. Although influenced to a degree by such classical composers as Frederick Delius,

77

Ellington's tone poems are in no sense derivative. Charlie Byrd's *Blues Sonata* (Offbeat 3009), Bill Evan's *Interplay* (Riverside 445), and George Russell's *Ezz-thetics* (Riverside 375) are among the growing number of serious jazz works in extended form which employ modified classical discipline. There are also many others that are simply jazz works extended by prolonged improvisation such as Sonny Rollin's *Oleo* (RCA Victor 2612) or suites made up of a series of loosely related themes such as *Gillespiana* (Verve 8394), but these do not so clearly reflect the encounter with the concert hall.

Recent Experiments

Gunther Schuller has perhaps done more than any other composer to combine jazz and classic idioms on terms that respect the integrity of both. His two sets of variations on themes by John Lewis and Thelonious Monk (Atlantic 1365) employ a string quartet and a jazz ensemble in an integrated and resourceful way. The same LP includes Schuller's briefer *Abstraction* and an appealing *Piece for Guitar and Strings* by Jim Hall, using a classical string quintet and jazz bass and guitar. Another Schuller work, *Conversation* (Atlantic 1345), blends the forces of the Modern Jazz Quartet and the Beaux Arts String Quartet; other pieces by John Lewis and Jimmy Giuffre on the same LP are also interesting but they alternate the jazz and classical instruments, never really integrating them. The same composers as early as 1955 produced a number of works for classical brass ensemble with jazz soloists Miles Davis, J. J. Johnson, and Joe Wilder. Although technically successful and intellectually interesting, Schuller's works are cold and detached; perhaps what is lacking is the warmth of the blues feeling in the Giuffre and Lewis pieces. But all of these works represent less than a decade of experimentation, and they show promise of what may later evolve.

Some of the most interesting experiments are those of André Hodeir, a classically trained French jazz theorist, whose *Jazz Cantata* sets wordless "scat" singing against a background of jazz instrumentalists (all French except drummer Kenny Clarke and trombonist Nat Peck) and whose briefer *Jazz et Jazz* utilizes electronically altered jazz-instrument sounds supplied by tape recorder (Philips 200-073). The result in these works is a tightly woven musical fabric — every note is composed; nothing is improvised — which is highly original as well as authentic in its jazz content, proving Hodeir's thesis that improvisation, though important, is not the essence of jazz.

Also symptomatic of the creative dialog between jazz and the concert hall is the career of Hall Overton. Known in jazz circles as a pianist and arranger, he can be heard performing works of Duke Ellington as a member of the Teddy Charles trio (Jubilee 1047) and has written a number of jazz pieces. In addition, four of his works in classical style have been recorded. Subdued jazz colorations are discernible in his Second Symphony, written in 1962 (Louisville Orchestra Society 633), which makes use of Afro-Cuban rhythms in its climax. Overton does not attempt the kind of fusion sought by Schuller, Hodeir, Russell, and others; the two realms are separate for him — but they are not sealed off from each other, and they reflect modes of expression for the same creative personality.

Jazz and American Culture

In a sense, this dialog goes on at other levels of culture, too, not only in music. Despite its stylistic cleavages and rivalries, the world of jazz is an interracial community; moreover it is above all a place where the Negro is not simply tolerated but looked to as the pacesetter — his contribution is incontestable. Throughout history, if we are to believe Arnold Toynbee, nations have achieved greatness through the intermingling of diverse cultures. Negroes in America have been exploited, ignored, taken for granted — even when, as individuals they have excelled in science, painting, or other fields of endeavor. Frequently Negroes are not excluded, they are merely omitted — from anthologies of American poetry, from films that do not have racial themes, from the boards of all sorts of benevolent agencies. As in popular music from Stephen Foster to Elvis Presley, the contributions of Negroes to American civilization (Banneker, Carver, Loewy) are quietly absorbed by a culture that continues to think of itself as white. Jazz by its whole history punctures this illusion. Once we begin to take it seriously and penetrate the façade of Paul Whiteman, Benny Goodman, and Dave Brubeck, once we begin to touch the creative sources, we are face-to-face with a challenge to the myth of white supremacy by which we live (whether we believe in it or not).

Somewhere behind the cardboard figures of Old Black Joe and the zoot-suited hipster, we find, a creative voice has been speaking. It has altered the course of European music as well as setting up bastions of freedom in Leningrad, Prague, and Warsaw. It is an American voice, but not the American of Plymouth Rock or Oyster Bay.

Whatever its inanities, the Jazz Age of the 1920s signified freedom — not for Negroes but for those white Americans who responded to the new if diluted idiom. Even the myth that jazz connoted primitiveness and that it was born in brothels at least served to call into question the other myths of puritan moralism that weighed so heavily in American culture up to World War I. Throughout the Swing Era this process continued and is epitomized in the simplicity and directness of the great pop ballads, contrasting sharply with the phony ostentation of prewar pop songs. But it is only with bop that the full impact was felt in freshets of linguistic improvisation that flowed into the mainstream of American slang and rapidly became absorbed into common usage.

The Impact of Jive Talk

The full story of linguistic renewal is outside the scope of this book, but it is a partial key to cultural vitality. All of us owe the familiar greeting "How goes it?" to a literal translation of the German immigrant's "Wie geht's." The major activity of this kind since the 1950s or even earlier has stemmed from the jazz world. "Are you with it?" "How are you making out?" "That's a far-out idea" — these are modifications of jive talk, which is a rapidly changing and highly inflected kind of verbal shorthand. There are ready equivalents in French for some of these terms, for example *"au courant"* for "with it" and *"outré"* for "far-out." In these respects, jazz-derived Americanisms have supplanted these linguistic imports and exhibited sufficient viability to displace them, for instance, in the English spoken in Great Britain, which formerly leaned far more heavily on gallicisms. What *"outré"* and "far-out" have in common is a hard core of meaning surrounded with a high ambiguity of implication. Such words have great expressive value and are very useful in suggesting rather than precisely stating a meaning. They give fluidity to language at a very immediate level, cutting through tedious constructions of more static terms. "Far-out" is equivalent to "outside the accepted conventional limits." We gain by reducing twelve syllables to two.

There is no exact identity between the argot of jazz musicians and the terms that pass into the mainstream, however. Some expressions are discarded by the former as they gain stability in the latter, and some of the cast-off terms become nothing more than dated slang. People who today continue to use words like "groovy" and "hep" are not with it; these words have been superseded. There is always a certain amount of lag here, with teen-agers picking up jazz slang virtually as soon as it is dropped. But a good many of the terms hold fast, become widely used, and are absorbed, gradually altering our speech habits and with them our conceptual equipment. One need only compare Henry James and Hemingway to see how 20th-century American English has become less a Germanic structure employing occasional French imports and more a language made up of more fluid parts. Hemingway would say "more intense" where James might use "intenser." If we appear to have lost thereby, we have nevertheless gained much through jazz — including the habit of easy coinage, of improvising a wide range of readily communicable meanings from such simple words as "cool" and "with it." Some of them have profound significance arising from the Negro's experience but transcending it — the use of "man" partly as an expletive but largely as a form of address not only is the Negro's retort to officious whites who have called him "boy"; it also engulfs all of our conventional postures from "sir" to "you there" and "buddy," making a semantic shambles of class and status. It is neither obsequious nor condescending, neither intimate nor aloof except as the speaker's voice may make it so by intonation. As an expletive ("Man!") it is certainly preferable in many ways to "gosh," "gee whiz," or "oh, dear."

Jazz Freedom and America's Destiny

This too, then, is part of the Negro contribution to America. As it has been absorbed it has become increasingly interracial, common to Negroes and whites alike, at each level. It is not a pose, though it may sometimes be used as such by some people; there is nothing inherently faddish or false about it. It is largely a natural adjunct to the habit of mind that goes with improvisation in music — but as it is an exercise of freedom it is also inevitably a form of protest against unfreedom, against rigidity and sterile conformity — particularly a protest against the unfreedom of a society conceived as a white man's world. There are expressions of bitterness; "ofay," pig-Latin for "foe," means "white." There are also expressions of defensiveness — but despite the abundant reasons for such attitudes the keynote remains affirmative: freedom for all rather than turning the tables. Both as a music and as the outlook that goes with it, jazz is an affirmation of man in his wholeness; it does not shut anyone out.

But it does not deny its roots, either. James Baldwin has articulated what is perhaps the core of the "jazz message":

> *White people cannot, in the generality, be taken as models of how to live. Rather, the white man is himself in sore need of new standards, which will release him from his confusion and place him once again in fruitful communion with the depths of his own being. . . . The price of the liberation of the white people is the liberation of the blacks. . . .*
>
> *In short, we, the black and the white, deeply need each other here if we are really to become a nation — if we are really, that is, to achieve our identity, our maturity, as men and women.*[2]

Jazz is, among other things, a powerful reminder that the American heritage is not an all-white heritage. Jazz is a ground of creative encounter in which Afro-American and Euro-American elements meet and blend. It symbolizes our mature identity as dehyphenated Americans. The message is not in the least incompatible with the fact that in a sense people are the same the world over — as is evident in the world impact of jazz — but it is right here that it most urgently needs to be heard and heeded.

5

POP MUSIC, JAZZ, AND THE CHURCH

There are many ways in which popular music touches on religion. A large segment consists of the popular musicians of the Bible Belt, whose music is fundamentalist in content, employing slick commercial arrangements of country-and-Western tunes or revivalist hymns with a sentimentalized piety that is raucous and pretentious. In these songs one often hears theological doctrines trivialized in stock phrases such as "saved by grace" when, to the accompaniment of twanging amplified guitars, they seem emotionally equated with "Rinso White." There are more than a dozen groups bearing the "gospel" label, from the Gospel All Stars to the Gospel Tones, and scores of others on such records as the Blackwood Brothers' *Pearly White City* (RCA Victor 2033) and the Sunshine Boys' *Golden Gospel Million Sellers* (Starday 156). As is the case with

84

secular pop music, the uncommercial backwoods religious music from which the "gospel hits" are derived is often beautiful and moving; a good sampling may be found on *White Spirituals* (Atlantic 1349) and on Obray Ramsay's *Banjo Songs of the Blue Ridge and Great Smokies* (Riverside 649).

There is a similar category of Negro gospel songs, some of which are as vulgarly commercialized as the above, with a parallel relationship to secular rhythm and blues. Yet quite apart from the authentic, unsophisticated Negro church, there are a number of independent Negro gospel singers and groups which, for reasons too complex to discuss here, have succeeded in resisting commercialism. Of these, Mahalia Jackson is the best-known example; others are Rosetta Tharpe, Clara Ward, and Ernestine Washington. A notable factor supporting this resistance is the crisscrossing of sacred and secular Negro music in the early blues and throughout the history of jazz. Many jazz vocalists such as Nina Simone, Della Reese, and Sarah Vaughan received their training in church choirs. Rosetta Tharpe is an example of one who subsequently returned to straight gospel singing after a stint with Lucky Millinder's band in the early 1940s.[1] Others, like Aretha Franklin, daughter of a Negro revivalist preacher, emerged from the church into rhythm and blues rather than jazz.

Within the mainstream of pop music, the encounter between the sacred and the secular has resulted in a bland, basically noncommittal piety, as vague in its way as fundamentalists are doctrinaire. Such singers as Pat Boone, Tennessee Ernie Ford, and Johnny Cash represent Bible Belt influences within the mainstream. More typical is Perry Como's *I Believe* (RCA Victor 1172) — and even this is a rarity, since few pop singers would risk a whole LP on religion. Most cheerfully avoid it in their entire

85

repertory except for a few standards, chief of which are Irving Berlin's "Easter Parade," "White Christmas," and "God Bless America." These are safe tunes; even the religion-in-general which they contain is minimal. Although the first two refer to the most sacred days of the Christian year, they say nothing about the Resurrection or the Nativity.

The goodwill of "White Christmas" is not that of the Prince of Peace; its cozy sentimentality is rooted in nothing more than nostalgia for the snow-blanketed scenes of childhood — "just like the ones I used to know." The songwriter is not a Christian, but in all candor does his vision of Christmas differ markedly from that of millions of uncommitted churchgoers?

Berlin's attention to the Easter hat "with all the frills upon it" is likewise no more a distortion than the fripperies which "Easter Parade" reflects. It is a mirror of actual churchgoers. If we examine these songs carefully both as to what they say and what they omit, and then consider how popular they are, it may not be too much to say that they simply help to perpetuate a startling misconception of the church.

"God Bless America" completes the picture of a genial, hedonistic culture. In contrast to the Bible, in which God transcends all nations, He becomes here a mere adjunct. The main focus is on America (ourselves), and God is called upon to "stand beside her and guide her" like an obliging pal. The spirit of the song seems to say that God automatically has to bless America because it is the "land that I love." Moreover, being patriotic (which is the same thing as good), I want to let God share in its glory.

All of these songs, from "I Believe" to "God Bless America," are in essence declarations of agnostic self-sufficiency rather than of faith. Unlike the commercial distortions of Bible fundamentalism, the content of these mainstream pop songs have nothing to do with the hymnals of mainstream churches or with even the most liberalized Christian theologies. If we add such novelties as "Rudolph, the Rednosed Reindeer" and " I Saw Mommy Kissing Santa Claus" and consider the fact that no doctrinally Christian pop ballad has yet come out of the entertainment industry, we may conclude that there is a wide gulf between its purposes and those of the church.

Liturgical Jazz

By contrast, in recent years there have been a number of attempts to place jazz in the service of the church, to awaken Easter-bonneted church people to the message of jazz or even to evoke religious motifs quite apart from the institutional church.

Perhaps the earliest use of jazz in a worship service dates back not much more than a dozen years, when the Rev. A. L. Kershaw, pastor of Trinity Episcopal Church in Oxford, Ohio, invited George Lewis and his Dixieland jazz band to play for his congregation. Rather than a structured liturgy, however, the Lewis band played classic blues such as "St. James Infirmary" and ragtime versions of spirituals. In July 1955, Kershaw appeared on the CBS-TV program "Look Up and Live" with a Dixieland group presenting "Religion and Jazz." Lewis' efforts may be heard on LP as *Jazz at Vespers* (Riverside 230).

It remained for Edgar Summerlin to make the creative breakthrough. Summerlin grew up in Lexington, Mo., near Kansas City, and as a boy listened to the big swing bands. But it was the advent of Parker and Gillespie that really awakened him. Although he pursued conventional studies leading to a master's degree from the Eastman School of Music, and showed ability as a composer in the classical idiom, jazz predominated in his thinking.

When his 9-month-old daughter died in 1958, he wrote "Requiem for Mary Jo" in jazz idiom as the most natural way of expressing his grief.

But it was his jazz setting of John Wesley's Order of Morning Prayer, premiered at the National Convocation of Methodist Youth in Lafayette, Ind., on August 28, 1959, that marked the first major liturgical use of jazz. Summerlin had studied with such men as Teddy Charles, Hall Overton, and George Russell, and their influence is evident in this work, which was soon recorded (Ecclesia ER 101) as *Liturgical Jazz* and has been played in a number of churches as well as on television. As recorded, the music is performed by a jazz nonet led by Summerlin, with the text spoken by Roger Ortmayer, professor of Christianity and the arts at Perkins School of Theology in Dallas. An attractive work with some fine improvised solos, it tends to be somewhat episodic, and the music and text are not always well integrated, a flaw due partly to the liturgical structure of this particular work.

Others meanwhile carried on the loose-knit "jazz at vespers" idea. At Christ Church Cathedral in St. Louis, Canon Standrod T. Carmichael presented a program of hymns and spirituals from "Rock of Ages" to "Joshua" played by the Singleton Palmer Dixieland Six, a local Negro band. In New York, John Gensel, pastor of Advent Lutheran Church, began holding "adventures in vespers," featuring Charles Mingus and others. Carmichael had hardly begun, however, when he started working toward something both more modern and more liturgical than the vespers. The result was his "Music for the Liturgy, 1961," which can accurately be called a jazz mass. Designed for a service of Communion, it consists of Kyrie, Sanctus, Agnus Dei and Gloria in English texts sung by the congregation and played by a jazz quintet. It has been recorded by Carmichael with a vocal group and the Saint

Louis Jazz Quintet, an integrated ensemble. Soon afterward, Carmichael produced and directed a musical revue, "For Heaven's Sake," which was premiered at Ann Arbor, Mich., in August 1961, featuring such pieces as "I Got the Gimme God Blues" and "He Took the Rap for Me." The following February, the jazz mass was performed in St. Louis at the opening session of the annual meeting of the National Council of Churches' Division of Christian Education. It has since been played in Columbia, Mo., Dearborn, Mich., and elsewhere, often with Cannonball Adderley's "Work Song" used as offertory following the mass.

The next major development came once again from Summerlin, who was beginning to achieve stature among first-rank jazz artists as a composer of depth and originality. His "Evensong," premiered at the Episcopal Church of the Epiphany on June 3, 1962, as the concluding event in a four-day International Jazz Festival held in Washington, D. C., gives convincing proof of creative gifts wedded to a trenchant musical intellect. Summerlin's nonet for this occasion included some top jazzmen — Don Ellis, Ron Carter, Charlie Persip, J. R. Monterose, Eric Dolphy, Barry Galbraith, Slide Hampton, Dick Lieb, and Lou Gluckin. The processional and the refrain of the recessional hymn were sung by the congregation and were written in simple ballad style to a text by the Rev. John G. Harrell with this use in mind. Following a relaxed instrumental prelude, soloists improvised unobtrusively as the processional was sung. Later, preceding the congregational reading of the Apostles' Creed, choir and instrumentalists performed a motet, "Song of the Apostles," with words beginning "Glory on that mountain, glory all around, glory be to Jesus, let's make a sound" — clearly of gospel-blues derivation. The offertory was an instrumental work composed in modified twelve-tone style with opportunities for improvisation — an excellent blend of advanced classical and jazz idiom. It not only deserves to rank among some of the best recent jazz works by itself, but this "difficult" piece fits admirably with the "easy" jazz hymns as well.

"Evensong" was subsequently presented on CBS-TV's "Look Up and Live" and at the Church of the Saviour (Methodist) in Cleveland Heights, Ohio, in April 1963 in conjunction with a Festival of Religion and the Arts. It drew a variety of responses. John S. Wilson, columnist for the New York *Times,* called it: "Dry, angular avant-garde jazz. . . . This was experimental music that still has a very limited appeal. . . ." Others regarded "Evensong" as a work of mature integrity. The masses of Machaut and Stravinsky also could be called dry and angular, with an even more limited appeal, and it would be hard to imagine even traditional hymns more readily accessible than Summerlin's. There is, nevertheless, a tendency among many people to identify worship with certain types of music, and this makes for a prejudice against the new and unfamiliar regardless of its intrinsic merits. Happily, Summerlin is not among those who feel that jazz requires an apology; in "Evensong," as in later works developed with Don Ellis and Don Heckman with the Improvisational Workshop Orchestra, he follows his creative instincts rather than approaching his listeners with condescension.

None of the works in this area produced during 1963 to 1965 are of a comparable stature. A possible exception is "A Musical Offering to God" by Thomas Vaughn and Charles Smith, a well-wrought conception unevenly executed in its premiere on September 29, 1963, at Advent Lutheran Church in New York City. Involving stylistic elements drawn from Ellington, Monk, and the gospel-blues tradition, it has moments of conviction but also contains arid stretches of effete Debussyan chords; as a whole it is not well integrated. Nevertheless, it is an interesting attempt, particularly for its experimentation in adapting influences from the Negro church to a modern jazz setting. It raises the problem of developing a religious jazz vocabulary, and this issue is one that is certain to be debated as further jazz liturgies are created. During the same year, jazz pianist Mary Lou Williams, a convert to Roman Catholicism, composed a jazz hymn to St. Martin de Porres, the first Negro to be canonized, which was performed at Philharmonic Hall in New York.

On November 10, 1963, overflow crowds thronged Westminster Presbyterian Church in Portland, Oreg., at 4:30 and again at 7:30 for a jazz version of John Calvin's Strassburg Liturgy of 1545, composed and arranged by Ernest Hood, a local musician. Written in the cool style for trumpet, valve trombone, alto and baritone saxes (both doubling on bass clarinet), string bass, percussion, and organ, it consisted of an original prelude and postlude with a blues-influenced offertory, as well as improvisations inserted into three congregational hymns: "Holy, Holy, Holy," "Once to Every Man and Nation," and "Son of God, Eternal Savior." Despite the hectic diversity of 16th-century liturgy, 19th-century hymns and 20th-century jazz, response was generally enthusiastic. According to Charlie Hanna in the Portland *Reporter,* "Hood's writing achieved a smoothness and urgency which was musically thrilling, but its religious significance could be anybody's guess." Dr. Robert H. Bonthius, minister of the church, said: "The response in hymn singing was tremendous. I think the liveliness and beat of the music really got the congregation involved." Another such service was held on May 3, 1964, with the jazz septet reduced to a quintet and adding an effective anthem, "The Brazilian Psalm," to the program with bass and percussion accompaniment. Although not as well attended as the November premiere, interest was strong enough so that Eskil Randolph, minister of music, proposed that the church hold one jazz service a month. Large numbers of the people who attended these services were not church members, nor were they musicians. These facts are not unique, but they caused Randolph to wonder — "What would be the difference if the musicians had church background and therefore would feel more sensitivity about the contribution jazz could make?" Such questions, of course, point to the basic rift between church and culture that is so characteristic of our times, and answers are likely to be found only through dialog and experiment.

On a Sunday morning in February 1964 a Dixieland jazz service was held at Spencer Memorial Church (Presbyterian) in Brooklyn. Although the tunes were chosen for their religious relevance (e. g., "Nobody Knows You When You're Down and Out"), the prevalent bouncy fun style, devoid of blues feeling, drew an enthusiastic response from the congregation on what seemed to me a shallow level. It was more a matter, as it turned out, of simply using the chancel as a place for a random good time — despite the earnest intentions of the capable white amateur musicians.

An "adventure in vespers" at Advent Lutheran on March 8 by Randy Weston was equally disappointing. This consisted of a series of highly polished commercial jazz compositions which, except for some good improvised solos by saxophonist Booker Ervin, were performed in a manner closer to Roger Williams than to jazz. These pieces were interspersed with Scriptural passages selected by Pastor John Gensel as relevant to the mood or title of each. Weston is capable of creating convincing jazz but inhibits himself in favor of mere technical display applied to pop formulas. Here again, the congregation (which overflowed all available standing room) was moved but at a shallow level.

In May 1964 "The Whole World in His Hands," a jazz mass by Bruce Prince-Joseph, was performed at All Saints Episcopal Church in New York City by a septet including such jazzmen as Teddy Charles and Thad Jones. The composer, a talented organ and harpsichord virtuoso, admitted candidly that this was his first foray into jazz. Understandably, the attempt was a sincere and reverent one, well-conceived but very limited in its success as jazz. It was chiefly notable for its direct borrowings from the Negro church: the offertory was the spiritual "He's Got the Whole World in His Hands"; the Communion anthem was "Let Us Break Bread Together." The Kyrie effectively blended elements of jazz and medieval plainsong and was followed by "Veni Creator Spiritus," which fitted in very well. The Nicene Creed was a syncopated chant over drumbeats, followed by "Balm in Gilead." Up to this point, the jazz effect was subdued and idiomatic. The offertory was sung by contralto Gloria Wynder in a style reminiscent of Odetta's, to a relaxed instrumental accompaniment featuring trumpet solos by Thad Jones. The remaining parts of the mass, however, were overcomposed and devoid of jazz content. The Sanctus sounded like an imitation of the classical composer George Rochberg; the Agnus Dei resembled a slick blend of Mantovani's ballroom sentimentality with a few Stravinskyan touches; the Gloria derived more from Milhaud or Stravinsky, still with a commercial overcast except for a brief passage toward the end which seemed to open up toward jazz expression.

During 1964 saxophonist-flutist Paul Horn and his quintet joined Fred Katz and cantor Alan Michaelson in a movement to place jazz at the service of the Jewish liturgy, improvising on Hebraic musical forms. At Horn's suggestion, Hollywood composer Lalo Schifrin wrote the first purported jazz mass based on the authorized English translation of the Roman Catholic liturgy. Scored for women's chorus and a large instrumental ensemble, it undoubtedly contains jazz elements, but the total effect is decidedly that of "pop jazz" of a hybrid sort — very clever and employing unusual devices effectively, but essentially commercial, relying more on effects than on improvisation or other creative means of expression. The Credo, for example, is chanted in a manner reminiscent of Darius Milhaud's *Les Choéphores*. The Sanctus uses strummed piano strings in the manner of Henry Cowell, but is otherwise big-band pop music with a bossa nova beat featuring a flute solo by Paul Horn that is — like much of Schifrin's music — derivative of Heitor Villa Lobos, Luis Bonfa, and others. It is an enjoyable work, but it lacks the "true voice of feeling" which is essential to jazz. Despite the sacred text, it conveys no more exaltation, mystery, reverence, or other religious attributes than does Schifrin's earlier *Gillespiana*. Moreover, it is overwhelmingly an instrumental composition in which room, and none to spare, is made for the text. When both chorus and band are playing, the words are more often drowned than buoyed. Although it may best be viewed as a departure from jazz rather than a contribution, it nevertheless deserves respect as a rare venture in its particular commercial idiom. It is hard to imagine its use in worship, however, and this perhaps contributes to the hybrid character of the work. It is clearly conceived for performance in a concert hall rather than in a church.

Liturgical jazz is still in its infancy. The problems it has to confront are many and complex, and they are chiefly of two kinds. For the composer and performer there is the key problem of finding an idiom that is both authentically jazz and suitable for worship. Merely to place a jazz ensemble in the sanctuary does not solve this problem, nor is it necessarily solved by choosing hymn tunes as vehicles for improvisation. There must be something more, a certain reverence of style that is easier to recognize than to prescribe. In part, no doubt, the difficulty stems not only from the contemporary split between church and culture but from the fact that most jazz players do not share in the life of the church. This is no simple matter in which blame can be assigned to one side or the other, but it does reflect the fact that, unlike Bach, the jazz musician is often involved in the church's life at this point alone, and he lacks an operational knowledge of liturgics as an "art of worship," not to mention its deeper meaning. Sacred music, whether congregational or otherwise, is a special art form with its own characteristic needs. I do not mean that it must cower in the shadow of tradition, but whether it extends or shatters traditional forms of worship, sacred music must have some way of comprehending itself as expressing the spirit which traditional forms have sought to express. The Prince-Joseph Kyrie, for example, finds points of contact between jazz and plainsong. Other composers have tried to capitalize on the syncopations in much of Bach's music. Summerlin's "Evensong" seeks to develop its own language, recasting traditional texts to accommodate jazz rhythms, and in the period since its premiere this composer has been seeking out serious religious texts in contemporary language, both poetry and texts conceived for worship as such.

From the church's side, perhaps the most noticeable problem is an emotional overinvestment in 19th-century piety and hymnody. Many of us do not realize that with very few exceptions the great hymns of St. Clement, Saint John Chrysostom, St. Francis of Assisi, and others come to us in translations dating from the 1860s, and even those of Reginald Heber and Isaac Watts have been subjected to 19th-century harmonizations. Morever, as Erik Routley has observed, our music directors and compilers of hymnals have conceded too much to sentimentality. Much of our hymnody is rooted in private or "in-group" emotional associations rather than mature musical tastes; we continue to savor our favorite hymns from Sunday school days, whether they have enduring value as music or not. In a surprising number of churches the congregation is unable to sing Bach and clamors not for instruction but for simple ditties learned in childhood. The response to liturgical jazz must be seen to some extent in relation to this problem. Those who resist jazz are most often those who would also resist Bach as an "innovation" — and they tend to be the older people, those for whom the "tried and true" hymns of childhood possess the richest emotional associations. It is no accident, incidentally, that so many of our grandparents' favorite hymns resemble the sentimental ballads of their day. "Onward, Christian Soldiers" and "The Lost Chord" came from the same pen that composed the music for *The Mikado* and *Yeomen of the Guard.* For much the same reasons younger church members may too readily respond to liturgical music patterned after "I Want to Hold Your Hand." In welcoming jazz, they may not be taking it as seriously as it deserves to be taken. And this points to a temptation for the musician to play down to the level of an undeveloped musical taste.

By the same token, novelty alone may attract the merely curious from outside the church, but something more is needed if jazz is to become a real medium for communicating the Gospel. This is true also for church members of every generation. Granted that accustomed ritual can lose its vitality, the mere presence of jazz in church does not guarantee its renewal. It may awaken the somnolent without thereby turning their thoughts to God, and only distract others who were already awake to God.

There is little likelihood that jazz will supplant the present forms of sacred music, either overnight or gradually. Despite the problems that go with it, however, the movement for liturgical jazz can be a healthy contributor to church renewal — partly by engaging the church in a challenging dialog and introspection regarding its existing forms of worship and partly by calling forth new efforts at hymnody in less flowery language and less fluffy musical idiom than the 19th century provided. The resulting hymns will not be jazz, perhaps, but they will owe something to it.

The foregoing are only sketches and guidelines. Liturgical jazz is still much too new for us to make detailed predictions about its future, except that there will be more of it, both good and bad, and it will take some time before the problems begin to be solved, canons of taste are formed, and rules of practice established. What, finally, is the optimum role of jazz in the church? Is it best for an occasional vesper service, for a Sunday afternoon ministry of music? How far can it go as a complete service of worship — presumably for a special occasion? Probably in the years ahead more atempts will be made to develop liturgical texts suitable for jazz use, and it is to be hoped that there will be closer collaboration between musicians and theologians. But beyond this, it is too soon to tell. As in every new and creative endeavor, there are risks and there is unpredictability.

Religious Jazz Outside the Church

Religious motifs are not something that has to be imported into jazz from the outside. From the time of Buddy Bolden to the present there have been jazzmen who spoke of "preaching the blues" on their instruments. The very name of the first important hard-bop ensemble is indicative: the Jazz Messengers. The gospel-oriented composition "The Preacher" (Blue Note 1518) by Horace Silver, the principal leader of this style, became a model for numerous hard-bop pieces such as Nat Adderly's "Sermonette" and Samuel Hurt's "Jackleg," the latter a slang term for an itinerant evangelist. Recent LPs in this idiom

97

include Les McCann's *The Gospel Truth* (Pacific Jazz 69), with versions of "Bye and Bye," "Were You There," and other hymn themes, Grant Green's *Feelin' the Spirit* (Blue Note 4132), and Jackie McLean's *Let Freedom Ring* (Blue Note 4106).

Outside the hard-bop orbit, Theolonious Monk has written a very brief and straightforward arrangement of "Abide with Me," featuring Coleman Hawkins and John Coltrane (Riverside 1102). A number of pieces by Charles Mingus combine serious musicianship with vigorous evocations of the Holiness church. Mingus attended as a child — "Wednesday Night Prayer Meeting" and "Moanin'" (both on Atlantic 1305), "Prayer for Passive Resistance" (Mercury 20627), and "Ecclusiastics" (Atlantic 1377). These and others possess all the "soul" of hard bop but surpass its stylistic limits. Mingus' "Revelations," dating from 1957, is a powerful 12-minute work combining near-classical composition with definite blues elements. It has been called "a celebrated evocation of the Deity" by critic Ralph J. Gleason; the work is featured in *Outstanding Jazz Compositions of the Twentieth Century* (Columbia C2L 31). The gospel-blues influence in Ornette Coleman's "The Blessing" (Contemporary 3551) and "Compassion" (Contemporary 3569), on the other hand, is scarcely noticeable, though there is evident a highly personal expressiveness that might be termed religious. In much the same category are Andrew Hill's "Judgment" and "Reconciliation" (Blue Note 4159).

George Russell's "Honesty" (Riverside 9375) can be classed with the Mingus evocations. More intriguing is his "Thoughts" on the same LP, which is far from hard bop but makes poignant and sparing use of the simple 6-note musical phrase corresponding to the words "down by the riverside" from the spiritual, "Ain't Going to Study War No More." It is not the mere quotation but the whole conception that gives this piece a meditative religious character. Sensitive jazz soloists in this recording are given scope for their own expressiveness — as they are in the Mingus and Coleman pieces — producing a rare and effective blend of compositional discipline and blues feeling. It is perhaps not irrelevant that both Russell and his principal soloists are Negroes, but it is worth noting that white players in his sextet also join in the spirit of the piece.

By contrast, John Lewis' *Original Sin* (Atlantic 1370) is "white" jazz by a Negro musician. There is nothing of the gospel tradition in it and for that matter little of jazz. Composed for symphony orchestra to a libretto by poet Kenneth Rexroth, *Original Sin* was premiered in 1961 as a ballet score accompanying scenes of Genesis from the Creation to the Fall, and was danced by the San Francisco Ballet. It is a bland, undistinguished work unworthy of Lewis' creative gifts, though undoubtedly it makes pleasant listening.

Little of a religious nature has come from the big bands. In the 1930s, according to jazz critic Stanley Dance, Jimmie Lunceford featured such pieces as "Lawd, Lawd" and "In Dat Morning" with bass player Moses Allen using his instrument to preach the sermon. Two of the finest works are portions of Duke Ellington's *Black, Brown, and Beige:* "Come Sunday" and a setting of the Twenty-third Psalm, superbly rendered by gospel singer Mahalia Jackson on Columbia CL 1162. It is fitting that of all the works of religious jazz outside the church, the latter is the most explicit in its statement and in its fusion of the separate strands of secular jazz and the church-rooted gospel singing. It is also characteristic of Ellington that it synthesizes elements of African and European derivation in a distinctive American way. It is ironic that religious jazz pieces have more often been heard in concert halls or in night clubs than in churches.

CONCLUSION

"The earth is the Lord's, and the fullness thereof." The creative arts are part of that fullness which man has fashioned from the bounty of God's creation. Music is one of these arts, and today's pop music and jazz are specific forms conditioned by history and geography. They are, in short, aspects of culture — the life of man in the order of created nature, in interaction with his fellowman and with his environment. Music, together with all of culture and of nature, is ultimately a gift of God. But the gift is not an outright one. Man possesses the power to destroy wantonly, to abuse or pervert or ignore this gift. But he does not possess the right to do these things. For the gift is part of God's covenant with man, and it is conditional upon man's rightful use of it; it is given to man for his rightful and beneficial use as an intelligent and responsible steward.

We would misplace our emphasis, however, if we were to draw from this only the conclusion that man must be preoccupied with responsibility to the exclusion of enjoyment. For enjoyment is the essence of a gift, and we miss the point if we regard ourselves as custodians or watchdogs rather than as recipients. We are not unaware of God as Lawgiver and Judge, but in and through Jesus Christ we know that God is Love. His creation is an act of love, as is His act of redemption in Christ. That is the "good news" which the Gospel embodies, and which the Holy Spirit manifests in the fellowship of believers, the church. Faith, hope, and love — these are the terms by which the apostle Paul designated the very core and dynamic of the church. They express an ultimate optimism predicated on an unshakable belief in the goodness and love of God. Even in adversity, rejoicing has always been the characteristic note in the church's proclamation of God's Word and its celebration of the sacraments.

Let us beware of smugness here. Much has been said in recent years to deprecate Pietism, the 17th-century movement of spiritual renewal which brought a needed emphasis on Bible studies and religious commitment, but which is also known for its strict ascetic attitude toward the world and for its suspicion of many forms of enjoyment. What we have noted earlier about Victorian attitudes should not be mistaken for a blanket repudiation of this honored tradition which spans from Spener to Kierkegaard. But Pietism, it is true, was attuned to the conditions of an earlier time; the world to which it addressed itself is not the world that we face today. We may tomorrow find ourselves in need of a new kind of Pietism — and it may not be too soon to start thinking about it even now. But with all deference to that prospect, the more urgent mandate is simply to regain the overarching theological understanding of the world and our place in it as Christians — and to apply this understanding not to some world of former times but to the world in which we live today.

This world is a world of rapid communication and social mobility, of urbanization and automation, of scientific discovery, of democratic freedom and bureaucracy, of mass consumption and mass conformity. One of the cultural features of this world is pop music, and we have seen how it has evolved from the petty commerce of penny ballads sold in the streets to a huge, hard-sell industry engaged in the manipulation of the emotions of a vast number of people. The first thing to be said about pop music today is that it is here, it is part of our world. To the extent that it is good, it is for our enjoyment. To the extent that it is bad, it is our responsibility as Christians to change it.

But first we should try to understand it. Uncritical acceptance or rejection is not good stewardship. Part of the purpose of this book has been to show the complex interweaving of the authentic and the crassly commercial in pop music. There are no surefire, hard-and-fast rules for determining whether a particular piece of pop music promotes neurotic daydreaming or legitimate escape. We have only indicated that such questions are applicable. It is up to each Christian to apply them and find his own answers. The doctrine of creation has positive relevance here, for it says: don't be afraid to enjoy yourself, even in a carefree way. Pop music doesn't have to be profoundly meaningful to justify its existence, and God does not require that every moment be profound. But don't be taken in either. Recognize the limitations of this kind of enjoyment, don't exaggerate its value, and don't give too much of yourself to it. And above all, consider your larger responsibility of stewardship.

This means cultivating standards of taste and judgment

102

and exercising them in the marketplace — insisting on a better product from the music industry, resisting the pressures of mass conformity. Most often this is easily done by choosing to buy the records you like best, regardless of their position on the best-seller list, and encouraging your friends to do likewise. But it can take other forms as well, by expressing your preferences in letters to disk jockeys or speaking out against music that is decidedly "sick" or trite or offensive. Just as in politics, you have only one vote, but it counts — and in this instance there is no age requirement. Your "citizenship" in the world of pop music comes to you by virtue of the fact that you are a listener and are thereby involved. God does not require that everyone must listen to music — but those who do must remember that they are heirs and stewards as well as listeners. They are in the world but not of it, and the standards by which they make their choices are not merely those of the world itself but are derived from an understanding of God's purpose for man's life. The Christian stands midway in the tension between the world as it is and God's higher purpose for it, shown in its created goodness. Music as such is good, but in some of it the goodness has worn thin or been twisted. You don't need to be a theologian to seek out the good, affirm and enjoy it, and resist the other.

Jazz, we have seen, calls for special attention partly because it has so often been misrepresented and misunderstood. The greater part of what makes the best pop music good comes through its borrowings from jazz or from folk music. But even at its best, pop music has the character of a commercial product fashioned at second hand from authentic human experience. As such, it is a lesser art. This is not to condemn it but to recognize its limitations and to point to the deeply rooted authenticity of jazz, which arose as a direct expression of a people's historic experiences and has long embodied a distinctive element of expressiveness in its performance. To be sure, there are examples of jazz so slick and superficial that they do not belong in this category, just as there are examples of pop music so authentic that they transcend their limitations. But in general, jazz by definition is a creative art form in which the musician does not merely perform to order but has something of his own to say — the joy or sorrow he communicates is not feigned but real, and consequently there is a sharing that does not occur in pop music. Moreover, jazz is characterized by freedom and risk. Its skill in performance goes beyond the technical dexterity required to execute a prescribed pattern of notes or even to utilize stock improvisational forms. For to a greater or less degree at every moment the jazzman must be ready to say something new, something distinctively his own. At every moment he is on call to respond either to his own inner promptings or to a musical statement from another player.

From its earliest days, jazz has been both nurtured by a sense of its past and driven forward by a creative need to grow, to avoid stultifying repetitions. Each great jazz player and composer has striven to find his own truest way of expressing what was in him and relating himself to his contemporaries, voicing both a personal and a communal response to life. There have been digressions into the exploitation of sheer form or technique, but, as in the bop movement, these have contributed to the quest for truer expression. The creative thrust of jazz is not merely a search for novelty, however; it carries with it an awareness of origins and traditions that has sometimes led it to seek to recapture elements of the past that seemed to have been lost, and to use them in new ways. We have also noted how jazz has proliferated into other nations and exercised a considerable influence on the major classical composers of our century.

In their encounter with jazz, Christians may embrace it as part of their culture, part of the goodness of God's created world. But unlike pop music, it is not merely a commodity designed for consumption; its purpose goes deeper than escape or entertainment. Listening to jazz is to partake of a form of human experience and to witness a dimension of ongoing creation in the world of culture.

There is no simple prescription for the understanding and appreciation of jazz except careful and attentive listening and perhaps a little study. The range of experience which it expresses may be broad, sometimes embracing meanings so subtle and personal as to be impenetrable to the listener, or too complex to be easily described in words.

The question of jazz in the liturgy is not decisive. The life of the church is not defined or exhausted by what happens on Sunday morning or at vespers or whether a clergyman or a church building is involved. Men and women are Christians by virtue of their relationship with God. Preaching, Bible study, sacraments, prayer and all that we think of as recognizably "sacred" or "religious" are special expressions of this relationship. But we do not cease to be Christians when we sit beside a radio or juke-box, or when we go to a jazz concert. We do not cease then to be "the church," even if we are far from the stained-glass windows and other accoutrements of our place of worship. We remember that the Gospel calls us not to withdraw from the world which God created but to participate in it and enjoy it. The earth *is* the Lord's, and the fullness thereof is His gift for our human benefit, for our creaturely good. It is not for us to ask that it be in perfect accord with our faith. What Paul said is as true of our generation of Christians as of his: "Whether we live or die, we are the Lord's." But the life we are given to live is in the world, and it includes the world of pop music and jazz.

QUESTIONS FOR DISCUSSION

1. How would you rate your church's attitude toward culture, especially the world of pop music and jazz? Victorian? Blind acceptance? Willingness to explore?

2. To what extent do you think the blues and gospel songs are results of slavery and discrimination? How much simply a matter of cultural differences?

3. Does the link between the blues and honky-tonks justify the moral stigma attached to them in the past? Considering all the facts, do you think this moralism may have been a rationalization for racial prejudice?

4. Which type of jazz do you find most congenial — New Orleans, swing, bop, or cool? Do you also find this type most meaningful and enduring?

5. Why do you think the Soviet government now tolerates jazz? Will this lead to other expressions of cultural or political freedom if it continues?

6. How would you evaluate the career of Stephen Foster? Was he a success or a failure? Are his ballads an important contribution to American culture? What about the racial stereotypes of such songs as "Old Black Joe"?

7. What do you think of the ballad "standards" of Gershwin, Berlin, Porter, etc.? How do they compare with current hits? How would you rate such Ellington ballads as "I Let a Song Go Out of My Heart" and "Mood Indigo"? Do they qualify as pop standards? As jazz?

8. What part of the "pop music spectrum" appeals to you the most? Which the least? Why?

9. How do you account for the tremendous success of rock and roll? Do you like it? Are there any significant differences between the Presley craze of 1955 and the Beatles craze of 1964?

10. Would you change your name to achieve fame as a pop music star? Would you go along with conforming to a standardized personality image?

11. Examine the lyrics of the current top ten song hits, separate from the music. How many of them employ neurotic fantasy? How many depend more on sound effects or styling? Which, in your opinion, are healthy in content, and why do you think so?

12. Is there anything that local churches can do to help provide alternatives to the night club as a place where jazz musicians can earn a living?

13. What do you think about "jive talk"? Are you aware of using it? Does it enrich or impoverish our language?

14. To what extent do you think the "new standards" to which James Baldwin refers may have roots in jazz? To what extent are they actually embedded in the Gospel? What is the relationship between the renewal of America as a nation and the renewal of the church as a community of faith?

15. Do you think jazz has a legitimate part to play in worship services today? In the future? Is this good or bad? What about hymns for congregational singing, such as those written by Edgar Summerlin? Is there a place in *your* church for Duke Ellington's setting of the Twenty-third Psalm or similar pieces?

NOTES

INTRODUCTION

[1] Karl Barth, *Theology and Church* (New York: Harper & Row, 1962), p. 347.

[2] Ibid., p. 343.

[3] Ibid., p. 344.

[4] Paul Tillich, *Theology of Culture* (New York: Oxford Univ. Press, 1959), p. 50.

[5] Nikolai Berdyaev, *The Meaning of the Creative Act* (London: Gollancz, 1955), p. 225.

CHAPTER 1

[1] LeRoi Jones, *Blues People* (New York: Morrow, 1963), p. 47.

[2] For example, *Thelonious Monk Plays Duke Ellington* (Riverside 12-201); Dizzy Gillespie, *Portrait of Duke Ellington* (Verve 8386); and the Teddy Charles Trio, *Three for Duke* (Jubilee 1047).

[3] For a good survey of "jazz internationalism," see *Down Beat,* Sept. 10, 1964. In addition to five articles on jazz in Europe and Asia, it includes eight pages of record reviews of Soviet, Brazilian, and European jazz groups.

CHAPTER 2

[1] "The Roots of Jazz" in Hentoff and McCarthy, *Jazz* (New York: Rinehart, 1959), p. 12.

[2] David Ewen, *Panorama of American Popular Music* (Englewood Cliffs, N. J.: Prentice-Hall, 1957).

CHAPTER 3

[1] T. W. Adorno, "On Popular Music," *Studies in Philosophy and Social Science,* Vol. IX, No. 1, p. 17.

[2] Ibid., p. 18.

[3] Paul Lussheimer, "On Daydreams," *The American Journal of Psychoanalysis,* XIV, No. 1 (1954), 86.

[4] Ibid., p. 88.

[5] Adorno, pp. 21 f.

[6] Harvey Swados, "Popular Music and the New Man of Skill," *Dissent* (Summer 1954), 272.

[7] David Riesman, "Listening to Popular Music," in Rosenberg and White, *Mass Culture* (Glencoe, Ill.: The Free Press, 1957), p. 411.

[8] Ibid., p. 413.

CHAPTER 4

[1] Igor Stravinsky and Robert Craft, *Dialogues and a Diary* (New York: Doubleday, 1962), p. 87.

[2] James Baldwin, *The Fire Next Time* (New York: Dial, 1963), pp. 110 f.

CHAPTER 5

[1] See Martin T. Williams, "Free Flow," in *Music '64* (Chicago: Maher Publications, 1964), p. 80. Also E. Franklin Frazier, *The Negro Church in America* (New York: Schocken Books, 1964), pp. 74 f.

FOR FURTHER READING

Charters, Samuel B. *Country Blues*. New York: Holt, Rinehart & Winston, 1959.

Dachs, David. *Anything Goes: The World of Popular Music*. Indianapolis: Bobbs-Merrill, 1963.

Ewen, David. *Panorama of American Popular Music*. Englewood Cliffs, N. J.: Prentice-Hall, 1957.

Feather, Leonard. *Encyclopedia of Jazz*. New York: Horizon Press, 1955.

Hentoff, Nat. *The Jazz Life*. New York: Dial Press, 1961.

Hentoff, Nat, and Albert J. McCarthy, eds. *Jazz*. New York: Rinehart, 1959.

Hodeir, André. *Jazz: Its Evolution and Essence*. New York: Grove Press, 1957.

  Toward Jazz. New York: Grove Press, 1962.

  The World of Jazz. New York: Grove Press, 1965.

Jones, LeRoi. *Blues People*. New York: Morrow, 1963.

Leonard, Neil. *Jazz and the White Americans*. University of Chicago Press, 1962.

Rosenberg, Bernard, and David Manning White, eds. *Mass Culture*. Glencoe, Ill.: The Free Press, 1957.

Spaeth, Sigmund. *History of Popular Music*. New York: Random House, 1948.

Stearns, Marshall. *The Story of Jazz.* New York: Oxford University Press, 1956.

Ulanov, Barry. *Handbook of Jazz.* New York: Viking Press, 1957.

   History of Jazz in America. New York: Viking Press, 1952.

Williams, Martin T., ed. *The Art of Jazz.* New York: Grove Press, 1959.

   The Jazz Tradition. New York: Grove Press, 1965.

. . . AND LISTENING

Background

African Coast Rhythms (Riverside 4001)

Negro Church Music (Atlantic 1351)

Country Brass Bands (Folkways FA 2650)

The Blues

Blind Lemon Jefferson: Folk Blues (Riverside 125)

Big Bill Broonzy Sings Country Blues (Folkways 2326)

Ma Rainey: Classic Blues (Riverside 108)

The Bessie Smith Story (4 LPs: Columbia CL 855/8)

Ragtime and Early Jazz

Jelly Roll Morton: Classic Piano Solos (Riverside 111)

King Oliver's Creole Jazz Band 1923 (Riverside 122)

Bix Beiderbecke and the Wolverines (Riverside 123)

The Young Louis Armstrong (Riverside 101)

The Louis Armstrong Story (4 LPs: Columbia CL 851 /4)

Fletcher Henderson & Duke Ellington: The Birth of Big Band Jazz (Riverside 129)

The Swing Era

Duke Ellington at His Very Best (RCA Victor 1715)

The Ellington Era, Vol. 1 (3 LPs: Columbia C3L 27)

Coleman Hawkins: Body and Soul (RCA Victor Vintage LPV 501)

Benny Goodmann: Carnegie Hall Jazz Concert (2 LPs: Columbia OSL 160)

Count Basie and Lester Young: Lester Leaps In (Epic LN 3107)

The Bop Revolt

The Harlem Jazz Scene, 1941 (Esoteric 548)
Charlie Parker Memorial (Savoy 12000)
Dizzy Gillespie: Groovin' High (Savoy 12020)
Jazz at Massey Hall (Fantasy 6003)
The Amazing Bud Powell (Blue Note 1503)
Thelonious Monk: Brilliant Corners (Riverside 226)

Post-Bop Trends

Miles Davis: Birth of the Cool (Capitol T 1974)
Miles Davis: Relaxin' (Prestige 7129)
Stan Kenton: Progressive Jazz (Capitol T 172)
Modern Jazz Quartet: Fontessa (Atlantic 1231)
Gerry Mulligan: Jeru (Columbia CL 1932)
Duke Ellington and John Coltrane (Impulse A 30)
Sonny Rollins: The Bridge (RCA Victor 2527)
Cecil Taylor Quartet: Looking Ahead (Contemporary 7562)
Ornette Coleman: Free Jazz (Atlantic 1364)
Bill Evans: Interplay (Riverside 445)
Charles Mingus: Mingus Mingus Mingus Mingus Mingus (Impulse A 54)
Thelonious Monk: Criss-Cross (Columbia CL 2038)
Jimmy Giuffre: Free Fall (Columbia CL 1964)
Jeremy Steig: Flute Fever (Columbia CL 2136)
Denny Zeitlin: Cathexis (Columbia CL 2182)
Archie Shepp: Four for Trane (Impulse A 71)

International Jazz

Gugge Hedrenius: Choose Now! (Swedish Columbia 1007)
Max Greger: European Jazz Sounds (German Brunswick 87918)
Karel Krautgartner & others: Czechoslovakian Jazz (Supraphon DV 10123)
Nikolai Gromin & Others: Jazz Jamboree '62, vol. 3 (Polish Muza 0396)
Friedrich Gulda: From Vienna with Jazz (Columbia CL 2251)
Golstain-Nosov Quintet: Leningrad Jazz Festival (Vee-Jay 2505)

Historical Anthologies

Thesaurus of Classic Jazz (4 LPs: Columbia C4L 18)

History of Jazz (11 LPs: Folkways 2801-11)

Encyclopedia of Jazz (4 LPs: Decca DX 140)

History of Classic Jazz (5 LPs: Riverside SDP 11)

History of Jazz (4 LPs: Capitol T 793/6)

History of Jazz: The New York Scene, 1914—45 (Folkways RF 3)

Outstanding Jazz Compositions (2 LPs: Columbia C2L 31)

Selected Pop Recordings

Ella Fitzgerald Sings the Cole Porter Song Book (2 LPs: Verve 4001/2)

Ella Fitzgerald Sings the George Gershwin Song Book (5 LPs: Verve 4029-5)

Ella Fitzgerald Sings Duke Ellington (4 LPs: 4010-4)

The Barbra Streisand Albums (Columbia CL 2007, 2054, 2154)

Frank Sinatra Sings Rogers and Hart (Capitol W 1825)

Great Jazz Artists Play Irving Berlin (Riverside 3519)

Great Jazz Artists Play Jerome Kern (Riverside 3516)

Great Jazz Artists Play Harold Arlen (Riverside 3518)

Andre Previn Plays Vernon Duke (Contemporary 3558)